M000284976

Empire and Righteous Nation

The Edwin O. Reischauer Lectures

Empire and Righteous Nation

600 Years of China-Korea Relations

ODD ARNE WESTAD

THE BELKNAP PRESS OF
HARVARD UNIVERSITY PRESS
Cambridge, Massachusetts
London, England
2021

First printing

Library of Congress Cataloging-in-Publication Data

Names: Westad, Odd Arne, author.
Title: Empire and righteous nation : 600 years of China-Korea
relations / Odd Arne Westad.
Description: Cambridge, Massachusetts : The Belknap Press of Harvard
University Press, 2021. | "Edwin O. Reischauer lectures"—
Series title page. | Includes bibliographical references and index.
Identifiers: LCCN 2020018584 | ISBN 9780674238213 (cloth)
Subjects: LCSH: China—Relations—Korea. | Korea—Relations—China.
Classification: LCC DS740.5.K6 W46 2021 | DDC 303.48/2510519—dc23
LC record available at https://lccn.loc.gov/2020018584

To the united and peaceful Korea of the future

CONTENTS

LIST OF MAPS

INTRODUCTION

For much of the past century, Korea has been forced toward the center of international affairs. In 1894–1895, China and Japan fought a war over Korea, each believing that control of the peninsula was essential to its own future. In 1910 Japan annexed Korea, seeking to incorporate it into a new empire. In 1950–1953, China and the United States engaged in a fierce conflict alongside their respective Korean allies, reducing much of the country to ashes. And in our own time, well after the Cold War, the North Korean Communist regime insists on its right to develop nuclear weapons and intercontinental missiles in response to what it sees as an American threat, making Korea—yet again—the center of international contention.

It is hard to reconcile the disasters Korea has been subjected to through foreign interventions with the remarkable advances the country has made when it has been allowed to progress by its own devices. Since the 1960s the Republic of Korea, which governs the southern part of the country, has become a manufacturing powerhouse, with some of the most rapid economic and social transformations ever seen. Today the South Korean GDP per capita is second only to Japan's among countries in eastern Asia and is one of the highest in the world—on a par with, say, Italy or Spain. Not bad for a country that a generation ago was in ruins!

It is easy, therefore, to conclude that Korea's most pressing current problems are by-products of its international affairs. And in spite of South Korea's material and social progress, there are many such problems. The continuing division of the country is at the top of the list, of course. But the complicated relations with China, Japan, and the United States also lead to difficulties both outside and inside of Korea itself. Some South Koreans fear that the country's future welfare may be endangered by its economy being squeezed, for political purposes, by its powerful neighbors. Or that the United States may strike deals with Beijing and Tokyo that are not to Korea's advantage. And, I think, all Koreans and most East Asians agree that any new war on the peninsula would undo not only Korea's economic progress but much of the economic advance of the region as a whole.

The stakes in Korea's current international affairs are therefore very high. If the Korean crisis can be resolved—and that, in my view, is predicated on the future peaceful reunification of the country—then eastern Asia's development into the world's center for growth and innovation is a predictable outcome. But if not, then the Damocles sword of unresolved tension will hang over any gain that the region will make, economically and politically. It is very hard to see how even the greatest of eastern Asian successes can compensate for an everlasting threat of war on the Korean Peninsula, now and in the future.

As I and others have been arguing for a long time, the main responsibility and potential for finding a solution to Korea's ills remain with the Koreans themselves. But given how the current situation came into being, it is also very clear that the Koreans alone cannot put an end to the country's predicament. They will need the assistance of neighboring countries, the United States, and the world at large. First and foremost they will need to work with China, the country's most powerful neighbor. And in order to engage China in a positive sense with regard to the Korean question, Koreans and others need to understand the historical background to China's involvement with the peninsula. An appreciation of the deeper past may help us see better what the alternatives are in the present. Or at least such an undertaking will enable us to ask better informed questions of policymakers and other leaders today.

This is, therefore, a small book about a very big topic. Its purpose is to explain to general readers how Korea's relationship with China has developed over the past 600 years. The focus on "deep" history is not chosen as a historian's extravaganza. I strongly believe that understanding long-term historical developments is essential for grasping today's international affairs, especially in cases where that history is not well known to an international audience. And given that Sino-Korean relations will be of crucial importance in the future, whatever happens in or around the Korean Peninsula, having some knowledge of what has happened in the past may help recognize new opportunities, or avoid false paths, over the years to come.

The book, based on the Edwin O. Reischauer Lectures delivered at Harvard University in 2017, presents an overview of Sino-Korean relations. Chapter 1 covers the time between the establishment of the Korean Chosŏn state in 1392 and the first Western incursions into Korea in 1866. It lays out how links between Chosŏn and Ming (and later Qing) China developed and the structural changes the association went through. It also discusses some of the key terms needed to understand relations between China and Korea, such as "empire," "nation," and "Confucianism." Chapter 2 deals with the dramatic changes the two countries went through from the late nineteenth to the late twentieth century, as imperialism, nationalism, and revolution refashioned states and peoples. It outlines how Sino-Korean relations metamorphosed through the era of Japanese aggression and the Cold War that followed. It also shows the disastrous impact the Korean War had on international relations in Asia. Chapter 3 introduces Sino-Korean interactions today and discusses some elements of the past that will be of particular importance for understanding future relations.

1

China and the Chosŏn State

The Making of Sino-Korean Relations, 1392–1866

China and Korea are neighbors, and there have been close relations between them for as long as there has been what could meaningfully be called "China" and "Korea," which is for at least 2,000 years. China is a big country, and for long periods of time its leaders have thought of it as an empire, a central state of many parts around which other countries and groups operate in various constellations relative to itself. Korea is smaller, but still quite large by most standards. With 85,000 square miles of territory, today's two Korean states are together roughly the same size as Great Britain, with a population of more than 75 million. Korea's inhabited regions have—and have long had—a very high population density, facilitating exchanges of goods, services, and ideas. China today borders fifteen other countries, and Korea has been its closest and most constant neighbor.

In terms of their social and political organization, both countries have had times of unity and disunity.[1] Even though, from the twentieth century on, nationalist historians have tried to delineate the antecedents of a unitary state as a historical norm, thereby making history a teleological account of national unification, there have been many different frameworks, at least up to the time when our story begins. Before the fourteenth century, China had had three eras of unification, the Qin / Han empires (roughly 200 BCE to 200 CE), Sui / Tang (600 to 900 CE), and the Yuan (1280–1370 CE). Korea had been united from the early tenth century in the Koryŏ state, but even before then a sense of Korean identity through language, customs, and (not least) food had spread throughout the peninsula. In their core areas, Chinese had thought of themselves as Chinese and Koreans as Koreans much before the late fourteenth century.[2]

In terms of culture, it is harder to find borders to delineate. In spite of differences in orientation, emphases, and connections, it makes sense to see China and Korea as part of *one* cultural region, at least from the Han empire onward. Confucian thinking, first emerging in China around 400 BCE, was established in Korea in the first century BCE, and Buddhism was introduced there through China 400 years later. The worlds of philosophy and religion overlapped to such an extent that it is sometimes hard to say where Korea ended and China began. There is a great deal of liminality and hybridity in the relationship, at least among elites: Confucian scholars born in Korea could work and teach in China, and Chinese-born Buddhist monks could join a temple or monastery in Korea. Identities could shift and change throughout one person's lifetime in a world where culture and beliefs most often trumped other forms of identity.[3]

One key link between China and Korea was the existence, since the arrival of Confucianism in Korea, of a common written language based on Chinese characters (what Koreans today call *Hanja*). This ideographic system, where each character has a distinct meaning but can be pronounced in whatever way suits the local language, became the official form of written Korean from the first century BC up to the Chosŏn era.[4] Even after Korea got its own alphabetic script in the fifteenth century, Hanja dominated as an administrative, religious, and intellectual written form of the language up to the twentieth century. This common world of literature and writing is of immense importance for relations between China and Korea, as it is for China's relations with Japan and Vietnam, which have also used Chinese characters as part of their writing systems.

Culture connected Koreans and Chinese, but state-building sometimes drove them apart. As China expanded as an empire, Korea's position vis-à-vis that entity became fraught. During the Han dynasty, Chinese leaders had attempted to integrate and assimilate Korean-speaking areas to become parts of the empire, just as they had (with greater success) other areas in the south (Nanyue and the Minyue, for instance).[5] But except during a limited period in Han times and a couple of generations under the Mongol Yuan empire, Korea had been outside of direct Chinese political control. One post-Han Korean-led state, Koguryŏ, had even attempted to rule over regions to the north and west that previously had been considered parts of the Chinese empire. China was at the center of cultural, economic, and political exchanges for Korea as it was for most of the eastern Asian region. But its ability to dominate Korea had been tenuous at best, and often nonexistent, right up to the establishment of the Ming empire in China in 1368.

The relationship between China and Korea changed under the influence of the new Ming empire and the equally new Korean Chosŏn state, which was set up two decades later. Just like the Ming in China, Chosŏn came into being as a reaction against the whirlwind of change that the Mongol conquests had subjected the region and much of the world to. In 1234 the Mongols had crushed Jin, the Jurchen-led state that bordered Korea in the west. Twenty-five years later they had defeated China's Song empire and conquered most of the country, setting up what they called the Yuan empire there to rule the eastern parts of their world conquests. Though headed by Kublai, Chingiz's grandson, the Yuan was led by a mixture of Mongols, Chinese, and others in an amalgam that made it a truly multiethnic empire, a bit like the Qing, founded by another group of Jurchens, were to become 350 years later. Also like the Qing in future years, the Yuan was an aggressive state, intent on further conquest. The Koryŏ state in Korea, which had been in control there for more than 300 years, was ground down by Mongol attacks. From the 1360s, parts of Korea were occupied by troops from the Yuan empire and Koryŏ lost its independence. Much of Korea was devastated by war and the Koryŏ state never fully recovered. When the Mongol global empires crumbled eighty years later, the Koryŏ monarchs were swept away too, replaced by a new dynasty intent on regaining Korean independence and further integrating the country. In both China and Korea the years under Mongol rule had meant brutal oppression as well as an opening to the outside world, through which new ideas could emerge and new concepts would take hold.

Empire

Before we look at that new, post-Mongol world as it came into being, it might be useful to explore a bit further some of the concepts we will be dealing with in this book. I chose the title *Empire and Righteous Nation* because it incorporates some of these key concepts: empire, nation, and righteousness. What do these terms refer to in a broader context and in the specific Sino-Korean relationship we will be investigating here?

Empire is a complex term, which has been around in an etymological sense in the Middle East and Europe for at least 2,000 years.[6] The form of state that the term describes has existed for even longer, probably since the Middle Eastern Akkadian empire around 2,300 BCE. The Akkadian rulers referred to their state as "bēlūtu"—meaning rule, dominion, possession, or control—and incorporated into it the basic building blocks of any empire: central authority and a systematic form of thinking to regulate the relationship between center and periphery. They also had most of the imperial apparatuses, cultural predominance and subject kings among them. The latter, it seems, are less important in generic constituent terms: Empires in history come in all forms and sizes, and there are many differences among them, including in degrees of cultural imperialism and levels of political subordination.[7]

For instance, some empires colonize, while others do not. England settled its own people in Ireland, forever changing the population character of that neighboring country. France attempted to do the same in Algeria.[8] Both of these colonized countries are in relative terms geographically similar to Korea, in the sense of being on the immediate borders of an imperial center. But in Korea, Chinese settlement has been very rare. The only real attempt at colonial settlement in Korea was by Japan, during the relatively brief period of its predominance there in the first half of the twentieth century, when more than one million Japanese settled on Korean territory.

In spite of the vast differences among empires, it may still make sense to speak in general terms of an Eastern and a Western archetype. The two imperial models would be the Qin / Han empire in China and the Alexandrine / Roman empire in the Middle East and Europe. There are similarities between the two, of course, but also differences. Both centered on the person of the emperor; each expanded in a short burst, followed by institutionalized empire that lasted a long time; both were highly militarized and centered on legal systems of universal application. But the differences are equally obvious. The Han were more ideologically oriented than the Romans. Han emperors were significantly more preoccupied with imperial integration and population settlement from the center. Both defined a core imperial area that future aspirants to predominance within each region would attempt to control, alongside an enduring written language, within which dreams of empire lived on across centuries. But only the Han left a geopolitical imprint and a language that serves a state today.[9]

The Han form of empire is recurrent in all Chinese empires over the past 2,000 years. There were variations, of course, in internal composition, ideologies, bureaucratic structures, and external strategies. Not least were there huge differences in economic form and purpose. Some Chinese empires (or states, when there was no predominant empire) encouraged trade and commerce, whereas others tried to limit or at least strictly control such activities. But in overall terms China has seen many attempts—some of them very successful—to imitate in form the Han model: a centralized, militarized state that demanded ideological conformity from the population and, in return, proclaimed that it would offer nurture, stability, and betterment to its people. Like the Han, all of them have emphasized hierarchy and, through that, bureaucratic governance. And all of them have asserted a sense of cultural centrality within the region, which was their known world, eastward toward Korea and Japan, and south toward Southeast Asia.[10]

In dealing with the outside world, some Chinese empires have been more expansionist than others. Following the Han model, the Tang and Qing empires expanded massively, including into parts of Central Asia that were well beyond the Chinese cultural sphere. Under the Qing, the empire grew to incorporate Manchuria and the northern Pacific coast (which the Manchu emperors held to be their ancestral lands), Mongol and Turkic states in today's Mongolia and Xinjiang (the empire's new western frontier), as well as Tibet and other areas in the Himalayas. Some of this expansion took place by long-planned conquest. But most of it happened as a result of security crises at the borders, to which the emperors reacted with massive use of force, taking control of territory far beyond any imperial blueprint made in Beijing. By the mid-eighteenth century, the Qing empire had become an enormous entity held together by bureaucrats and officers from many different groups and nations.[11]

Given their multiethnic character and the vagaries of both nomadic and settled forms of existence, the Chinese empires' border zones were porous and vague. Sometimes the definitions of what was inside the empire and what was without were unclear and ambiguous. Local leaders could appeal to become part of the empire for their own protection or economic gain. Others could set themselves up as kings or princes, grabbing a high degree of autonomy, especially when the empire was otherwise engaged. Clear lines of definition were often avoided, because such elucidations could create unnecessary conflict. Within a Confucian setting, where acting correctly while respecting hierarchy was the center-point of all diplomacy, some degree of indeterminacy could serve the interests of all sides well.[12]

Chinese empires increasingly used the term *tianxia* to refer to the polity they represented. Literally meaning "under heaven," the term has been used at different times in Chinese history to present universalist claims—all lands, "all under heaven," are subservient to the emperor—or to identify those places that are, or should be, under the emperor's control. The latter is, first and foremost, a civilizational claim: Peoples who have been civilized by Chinese culture belong within the empire or in some form of defined relationship to it. Others are "outside," beyond the realm of cultural identification and possibly beyond civilizational redemption, either because of their physical and mental composition or because they are too far away to meaningfully be incorporated into a Chinese-ordered world. The universalist and particularist definitions of *tianxia* have been contested throughout Chinese history.[13]

For those countries, such as Korea, that were not inside the borders of the empire, other forms of reflecting a *tianxia* order had to be found. Usually these consisted of forms of subservience expressed through intermarriage, hostageship, or gifts presented. Also, the terminology through which China's suzerainty was recognized and expressed was of extreme significance within a worldview as hierarchical as Confucianism. Sometimes presented as a "tribute system," this Chinese approach to dealing with neighbors was less than systematic and more than tribute.[14] During each of China's empires, court officials attempted to find the correct ways of expressing the empire's relationship to specific neighboring polities, using terms such as *fan* (vassal) or *gongguo* (tributary).[15] In reality, given the vagueness of ethnographic and geographic knowledge, the same country could have different designations, depending on when and how their representatives had been in touch with China. The key element, from the imperial point of view, was subservience, in words as often as in deeds or goods.[16]

It is important, however, also to understand how an imperial order looked different when seen from the periphery. Even the concept of periphery might be contested—there were times, as we shall see, when parts defined as peripheral by the empire defined themselves as central, or at least vital, to the Confucian order. But most commonly the rituals defined by the empire, including in personal behavior or through gifts, could in practice be defined differently when executed from outside of China.

All forms of ritual interaction with Chinese empires opened up opportunities for enrichment through trade or knowledge of new technologies, fashions, or foods. What was seen by the empire as subordination could sometimes be seen as concessions by those on the other side of the border.

As we shall see, Korea was, and had been for a long time, a distinct entity in the eyes of Chinese officials, different both from what was within the empire and from everything else that was outside it. Maybe the best way to express the relationship in Chinese terms is to call it something along the lines of "closest neighbor" or "most favored vassal." Korea was a constant for people within Chinese empires, in ways in which the peoples of the northern steppe, the western mountains, the southern jungles, or the eastern islands were not. It was a defined population within a reasonably set territory. Enough was known about the Koreans to define them as others, but others who stood in a close relationship to self. They were civilized (*hua*), not barbarians (*yi*), even though they by tradition did not fully partake in the blessings of imperial governance.

The two Chinese empires covered in this book are the Ming and the Qing. The Ming empire ran for almost 300 years, from the 1360s to the 1640s. The Qing were in power from the 1640s to 1912, also for almost 300 years. These are two long-lived polities by any standards, even China's. They had much in common, but also differences. The Ming was a homegrown empire, constructed as a reaction against foreign rule and excesses during the "savage" Yuan. It claimed to act on behalf of Confucian certainties and the cultural inheritance from the Song empire. It emphasized education and self-improvement among officials, as well as the study of the Chinese classics. It reinforced the Song principles of imperial examinations and layered bureaucracies. But, as Timothy Brook has stressed, in spite of their self-representation the Ming were also a product of the immediate past, meaning the Yuan empire itself. Ming emphasis on autocracy and the power invested in the person of the emperor was more reminiscent of a Mongol khan than a traditional Chinese ruler.[17]

The main reasons the Ming finally got into terminal trouble in the early seventeenth century need not detain us here. But it is worth noting that the program of the Qing conquerors was, again, to reinstitute Confucian correctness. This time the complaint was not against excess and barbarity, but over corruption and weakness in the imperial system. The Jurchen, a northeastern tribe who from the early 1600s began referring to themselves as Manchu, had ruled the Jin state that the Mongols had crushed in the 1230s, before Chingiz Khan's successors had turned on China and Korea. Four hundred years later it was the Manchu, and other groups that had joined with them, who issued a program for conquering China and reinstating ancient mores and procedures that they claimed had been forgotten under the irresolute Ming. The empire they called Qing, "clear" or "pure," but also "purify" or "purge," was deeply preoccupied with ritual and propriety. In spite of the strong suspicion and hatred they aroused in many Chinese as "outside" conquerors, the Qing saw themselves as the great systematizers of the Confucian tradition, with the might and will to protect and promote it.[18]

The Qing rose to power in eastern Asia just as European empires started to expand outside of Europe. All these early

15

modern empires had much in common, it could be argued, at least in terms of military organization and logistics. The Qing created an eastern Asian region centered on itself just as Spain, Britain, France, and Russia expanded in Asia, Africa, and the Americas. If there ever were a Chinese empire that wanted to organize its neighbors into a fixed system of hegemony and control it was the Qing. The instruments it used were military, diplomatic, cultural, and economic. Ironically, Qing leadership could often be described in ways reminiscent of John Gallagher and Ronald Robinson's "informal empire"—a term that is of course often used of British control in China during the late nineteenth century.[19] The Qing empire's tools were not primarily economic but culturally and ideologically coercive, with the threat of military force ever-present.[20]

The spectacular rise and fall of empires on a global scale over the past 300 years is much of the immediate backdrop for this book. In the nineteenth century, empires were on a high globally. Intense competition among European powers for wealth and influence led to a further carving up of Africa and Southeast Asia. By 1900 every corner of the globe was affected by European imperialism; one empire—the British—proclaimed that it covered more than a quarter of the world's landmass. By then, the United States and Japan had joined in the scramble, and so, to some extent, had the Qing, even though the Qing empire itself had been the victim of foreign imperial expansion since the Opium Wars. The Qing attempts at translating its former imperial predominance in eastern Asia into forms of European-style imperialist control is a topic we will return to later in this book.[21]

Nation?

When I speak of nation in this book, I am speaking of Korea. The Ming and Qing were many things, but nobody can imagine them as nations. They were empires, or *daguo,* if we so wish, with many groups within them, under one predominant elite and culture. But does it make sense to speak of pre-twentieth-century Korea as a nation? As with concepts of empire, concepts of nation are contentious. Even more than with empire, some historians and social scientists believe that any use of the concept outside of its European setting from the nineteenth century on is faulty or even perilous. It may be seen not just as anachronistic, but dangerously inaccurate, in the sense that it gives credence to nationalist myths created in the twentieth century and the aversion toward others that often goes with such ideas.

And, even so, the great coherence in forms of identity expressed by people on the Korean Peninsula over a very long time, and their relative cultural homogeneity, have led other historians to argue that Korea had developed forms of national consciousness well before any other part of eastern Asia. The great historian of Korea JaHyun Kim Haboush, who places the origins of Korean nationalism around the war with Japan in the late sixteenth century, explains it well: "I decided," she says, "to put forth the thesis of the emergence of a nation because I feel that the term "nation" is the most suitable frame for a historical phenomenon of such intensity and passion extending through the totality of Korean society and persisting through several centuries, not because I wish to determine whether the Korea of the premodern era was a nation by the criteria of bifurcated paradigms."[22] She treats Korea as having had a unique discourse of nation simply because there is no other term in English that seems to fit Korean perceptions and sensibilities with the same degree of suggestiveness and poignance.

Because it is clear that the question of Korean nationhood pre-twentieth-century is a troublesome one, a few historical accounts have eluded it by simply pointing to the great fusion in customs and language of people who live on the Korean Peninsula, a process that in linguistic terms goes back at least 2,000 years. Modern Korean language derives from Middle Korean, which in turn derives from—you guessed it—Old Korean, which has its root in some form of Proto-Korean before the 4th century.[23] But this is a typical historian's cop-out. Not everything that is distinct becomes a nation, in any meaningful sense of the term. In order to establish at least a worthwhile debate on the question, it may be necessary to provide a brief detour into the wrangle over concepts of nation and nationhood in a more general sense.

A much used definition of nation is that it consists of a large body of people united by common descent, history, culture, or language, inhabiting a particular state or territory.[24] The key aspects may very well be the emphasis on "something in common," and "co-location." It is very hard to imagine a nation that does not at least have at least one of the above myths or customs in common. Likewise, it is difficult to think of a nation, at least up to the cyber-age we have entered into now, that does not share some form of territory. There have, of course, been constant attempts at making religion or physiognomy into forms of nation, but these have always been heavily contested. For most people, there seem to be more to nationhood than saints and looks.

The complexity of the discourse on nation is of course connected to its specific origins in nineteenth-century Europe.[25] Some of these origins are to be found in the romantic reaction against the European Enlightenment: A search for collective authenticity, identity, and purity beyond the emerging rationalities that established state formations could offer. The promise of democracy was often part of this ideal, as was the idea of social reform; only a defined people, a nation, could practice democracy or develop social welfare, revolutionaries such as Italy's Mazzini thought, because only the nation would "give them a name, education, work, and fair wages, together with the self-respect and purpose of men."[26] The under-lying idea, of course, is that the "nation" necessarily and by right had to constitute itself as a political community, a "nation-state," to serve the people who lived in it. Ernest Renan summed the romantic view up well in 1882: "A nation is a soul, a spiritual principle. Two things, which in truth are but one, constitute this soul or spiritual principle. One lies in the past, one in the present. One is the possession in common of a rich legacy of memories; the other is present-day consent, the desire to live together, the will to perpetuate the value of the heritage that one has received in an undivided form."[27]

But there is also another nineteenth-century European view of the nation, which brings it much closer to both contemporary and past forms of empire. In France, where the revolutionary concept of an all-encompassing, democratic nation was pioneered, Bonaparte quickly transformed the revolutionary state into an empire, which throughout the century competed with other European empires, some of which were increasingly democratic and based on a national idea: Britain, Germany, Italy. "Is imperialism simply nationalism under another name," asks the Trinidadian sociologist Krishan Kumar. "Or nationalism no more than a continuation—again under another name—of the imperial impulse that preceded the rise of nationalist ideologies?"[28] Eugen Weber, of course, reminds us that "the famous hexagon [i.e., today's France] can itself be seen as a colonial empire shaped over the centuries."[29] "Were not all nations empires once?" asks historian Charles Maier.[30]

The process of interrogating the concept of nation may also go beyond issues of how "people" and "territory" have been historically constructed. For some scholars, following in the footsteps of Ernest Gellner, nationalists create the nation, not the other way around. Nationalists want to produce a congruence of the national (as defined by them) and the political, so that the two are overlapping entities. Thereby they attain ideological hegemony, power, and influence. Nationalisms as ideologies thrive under particular socio-economic conditions, and the nation is the outcome of such spectacular dreams, most often formulated by intellectuals. Behind every successful nationalist movement, claim some of my eastern European friends, stands a half-crazed historian.[31]

The form that nationalisms and nations take is therefore contingent on the moment of their creation. In many cases, especially in Europe, "nation" has been about exclusion, about who did *not* belong. In others, such as in postcolonial states, "nation" has been about association and encompassment, an attempt to include various groups within a political project that claimed to be some form of nation-state. Each process can be very contested and violent, and have led to removals, subordinations, and mass-killings.

For Korea, the exclusionary or rather definitional aspect of nation has played an important role. As Haboush and many contemporary Korean historians explain it, the discovery of Korean identity in a national sense took place when the country was under immense pressure by its neighbors, China and Japan. The process was, at the outset, definitional: Koreans did not, or at least not necessarily, belong within China or in subservience to Japan. Just like there was an empire in the north and west, and there were powerful leaders in the eastern islands, there was a Korea on the peninsula. This Korea was primarily defined culturally and linguistically, but had significant political and even institutional claims. What took place in early Chosŏn was very much a national discourse, with somewhat similar content to what would be seen later in Europe and the postcolonial world (not to mention in China and Japan).

This said, one should of course be careful with not exaggerating similarities or reading history backward. Just like "empire," "nation" *is* a European concept, fashioned, in its contemporary form, for specific nineteenth-century uses. Koreans in the fifteenth and sixteenth centuries would refer to their homeland as a country, *guk,* meaning both people and territory.[32] The specific European connotations of "nation" did of course not affect them as they tried to make sense of the situation they found themselves in. While employment of terms and discussion of similarities may be enlightening, one should be very careful with not building this into parallels beyond the historical material available.

Likewise, one needs to be aware of the massive differences there are between Korean nationalisms in the twentieth century and before. The intensity of nationalism in Korea over the past one hundred years tend, in many ways, to obscure earlier processes. Because it is so important to many Koreans today to make their nation ancient and significant, the very observation that Korean concepts of nation may indeed precede those in other countries can easily be buried under an avalanche of bad history and dubious claims. From the twentieth century on, Koreans have adopted European concepts of nation and have adapted them, sometimes ahistorically, to their own past. In some cases these undertakings seem entirely unaware of recent historical change or outside influences. The task, then, becomes to rescue what is notable in Korean history from inflamed versions of the twenty-first-century nation.[33]

Righteous

The third word that may need explanation is the term "righteous," 義 (yì in Chinese, ŭi in Korean). In Confucian thinking the term also implies moral fitness, loyalty, and fidelity to principles.[34] In applying this term to Korea (or rather Korean political projects) I do not at all intend to imply that most Koreans are exceptionally righteous or even particularly preoccupied with righteousness. I have just been struck by how often in Korean history righteousness has been proclaimed as the ultimate good or held aloft as a banner against oppressive regimes, domestic or foreign. The Korean armies that were raised against Japanese occupation in the 1590s and against Manchu invasions a generation later were all referred to as "righteous armies" (*ŭibyŏng*), as were those who fought against colonization in the early twentieth century.[35]

The connection, I think, serves as a useful link to the centrality of neo-Confucian thinking in Korean history over the past 600 years or so. What we know today as neo-Confucianism emerged in late Tang China and was fully developed during the Song empire in the eleventh and twelfth centuries.[36] The ostensible purpose of this direction in Chinese thinking was to free classical Confucianism from Buddhist and Daoist influences that had polluted it over the centuries and rebuild it as Confucius had intended. In reality, many of the ideas that emerged were new, at least in form, and helped link Confucian thought to a set of principled and practical rules for how civilized men should live their lives. Neo-Confucianism, it could be said, was a rationalist ethical philosophy for a new stage in Chinese history.[37]

There were a number of great thinkers who developed neo-Confucian ideas during the Song empire, but the most important systematizer was Zhu Xi, who was born in 1130 in the mountainous province of Fujian on China's southeastern coast. As an imperial official Zhu was less than a success, but as an analyst, harmonizer, and codifier he is perhaps the most important figure in East Asian history. Without disregarding the cosmological constructs of classical Confucianism, he managed to link knowledge, morality, and governance together in forms that have influenced China, Korea, and Japan up to today.[38]

The human world, according to Zhu Xi, originates in the Supreme Ultimate (*taiji*), the highest principles of existence, which were there before any community was formed. These principles are not active or God-like, but have been embedded in all humans along with the ability to cultivate them. Man is therefore born good, but needs culturing in order to know and subsequently act upon the principles that derive from the Supreme Ultimate. We must first know the material world through empirical examination before we can act rationally and morally. Education is needed to put matters in their proper place and thereby create good societies and good lives.

Zhu Xi's philosophy emphasized the centrality of the state and the emperor in enabling people to know the correct principles and therefore act rationally. In his enormously influential commentaries on the *Lunyu* (Confucius's Analects) and on *Mengzi*, both completed in 1177, the correct principles for governance are underlined throughout. Elsewhere in Zhu's gigantic literary production the principles of leadership are further developed. In "Outline and Digest of the General Mirror" (*Tongjian gangmu*) he uses historical cases to illustrate his positions, drawing on the work of the erudite Song historian Sima Guang. But it is in his commentary on the *Daxue* (Great Learning), a text on righteous government, that the hierarchical and integrationist impulses in neo-Confucianism are laid out in full. The emperor's personal character, Zhu asserts, is the basis for the well-being of the state. By cultivating his own mind, a leader will by necessity transform society and everyone in it and assist the world in moving closer to the principles coming out of the Supreme Ultimate.[39]

Zhu Xi and the neo-Confucians who followed him taught that righteousness means the propriety of things, a correct order in the family, society, state, and the world. Knowing the correct order is necessary in order to act correctly. Righteousness in Zhu Xi's neo-Confucian tradition therefore has two aspects, joined together through evidence of good results. One is knowledge of principles. The other is what Chung-ying Ch'eng calls "a decision-generating ability to apply a virtue properly and appropriately in a situation."[40] The neo-Confucian canon that Zhu Xi created was intended to represent the correct order of things and therefore spur men to righteous action.

Song era neo-Confucianism had a tremendous impact in China as well as in Korea. During late Song and Yuan, Zhu Xi's version attained increasing importance. And in the early Ming empire, the state gradually began employing neo-Confucian thinking to set the direction for its rule. By the early fifteenth century Zhu Xi style neo-Confucianism had become Ming orthodoxy, and—even if challenged and revised at times—it remained the heart of Chinese thinking about the world and about the state's role in it up to the late nineteenth century.

In Korea neo-Confucianism played, if anything, an even greater role, especially for the state. Forms of neo-Confucian thinking had reached Korea during the Koryŏ era and were much discussed there. Zhu Xi's reasoning about the state and its role in promoting correct forms of living was part of the inspiration for the men who constructed the Chosŏn government. From the very beginning, Chosŏn therefore became, as we will see, a neo-Confucian project, in which the purpose of the state was to promote virtues and banish errors. Principles of righteousness seem to have played a particular role in Korean neo-Confucianism from the beginning, linked to concepts such as morality and fidelity, which were highlighted by the Chosŏn regime.[41] *Ŭiriron*, the doctrine of righteousness, was a much used and much debated position for Korean officials and scholars on matters from the relationship with China to the ownership of land and the role of the king in the Chosŏn political system.

By the early part of the sixteenth century, much of the most poignant debate on neo-Confucian theory took place in Korea. Some of it was transmitted to China and elsewhere. Philosophers such as Yi T'oegye (1501–1570) and Yi Yulgok (1536–1583) engaged in extensive and sophisticated debates on ontological questions, among them the origins of human emotions and desires and how they may have emerged from the Supreme Ultimate.[42] But first and foremost neo-Confucianism gave purpose and meaning to the Chosŏn state. Even the titles of officers and officials were full of declarations: One general's rank was termed "general for safeguarding righteousness." Three ranks below appeared a "commandant for cultivating righteousness." And the King's personal garrison was named "The Righteousness-Flourishing Capital Guard."[43]

At least for the purposes of this book, it is important to be able to criticize all ideologies and stated motives. There is no doubt that neo-Confucian orthodoxy, in Korea as well as in China, became stale over time and lost the potency and urgency of the early Ming and Chosŏn eras. But, in both countries, it is also striking, over the years, just how much effort and aspiration went into reforming the dominant ideology and make it relevant for one's own times. Part of the reason for this is that

Confucianism had become an integral part of what Chinese, Koreans, and many others saw as their own culture. Understanding what it meant to be Korean or Chinese was impossible without understanding Confucian principles. They connected the two countries, and sometimes drove them apart through different understandings or applications of the same principles.[44]

The Ming and the Chosŏn

In the late fourteenth century both China and Korea went through profound political changes that were to determine their history over the coming 500 years. As Mongol rule crumbled, a series of rebel movements in China competed for supremacy. The one that came out on top was led by Zhu Yuanzhang. Born a peasant in Anhui province, Zhu became a remarkable military commander of a Chinese rebel group calling themselves Red Turbans. By 1360 he had set up his own splinter band under the name of Ming, meaning "bright" or "brilliant." Eight years later, after having defeated most rival rebels, he made himself Emperor Hongwu of the Ming Empire, with its capital in Nanjing. By 1381 the Ming was in control of China, having subdued all rivals and vanquished the Mongols.[45]

It is a remarkable story, one for the ages. But as remarkable as Zhu's path to power was his choice of using neo-Confucian doctrine to solidify his rule. The uneducated Hongwu emperor was a famously short-tempered man, with a particular dislike of scholars who wanted to lecture him on correct policies. But he realized that his new empire needed a justification and a social glue to keep it together, beyond the task of ridding China of Mongol rule. This Hongwu found in neo-Confucianism of the late Song era. It connected him and his rule to the Chinese past and it could be made to stress the obligation all scholars and officials had to serve the state. Its hierarchical emphasis on qualities of leadership could be turned into a justification for authoritarian rule, the way Hongwu liked it. While strictly regulating the activities of scholars and the rest of society, and employing great brutality in doing so, the Ming emperor had found an ideological instrument he believed both sanctioned his rule and improved China.

In spite of their insistence at being a clean break with the Yuan past, Ming emperors overall inherited more Mongol approaches to government than they liked to admit. Hongwu and his successors behaved more like khans than emperors of earlier dynasties. They were autocrats who attempted to assume personal control of all parts of the bureaucracy and institute a form of rule centered on the imperial family. This extreme centralization often made effective government more difficult, since everything depended on the emperor's personal qualities. But, ironically, it may have made it easier to accept a new kind of foreign relations, in which non-Chinese entities were connected to the empire's center through a variety of arrangements focused on the emperor. It added to the arsenal of diplomatic tools the empire had at its disposal.

For Emperor Hongwu, who ruled for thirty years, the priority was to restore the central parts of the empire and secure what he considered China's borders against foreign encroachment. But he also wanted to establish correct relations with the empire's frontier regions, and sent messengers to Korea, Vietnam, Thailand, Burma, and the Central Asian regions proclaiming his accession and the founding of the Ming empire. This was a tricky task: Hongwu did not claim the empire by inheritance but by virtue of conquest. The mandate of heaven had been bestowed on him through his success in battle. Even the reign name he chose for himself, Hongwu, meaning "Vastly Martial," announced the basis for his assertion.

The problem for early Ming foreign relations was that there were few set precedents for the subordination of neighboring countries, except those that came through the Mongols (unacceptable) or the Song tradition (by now very distant). In addition, Ming officials seem to have sensed that convincing those neighbors who had adopted significant parts of Confucian learning of the legitimacy of the imperial accession of a former peasant from Anhui might be difficult. The strength of the claim lay mainly in two factors, they knew: The sheer power of the Ming state, even in its infancy, and the idea that the new dynasty was truly Chinese, not Mongol, Turkic, or Tungus.[46]

When Hongwu first turned to the Koryŏ kingdom in the early days of the Ming in order to establish relations, he was therefore very cautious. Even though there is no doubt that he wanted Koryŏ to subordinate itself to Ming, he phrased his approach carefully:

I have become emperor of China from a humble background, and have received the submission of foreign kingdoms in the Eight Directions, which are living in tranquility with one another. They have not wantonly disturbed our frontier, and

I have not rashly resorted to pacifications. Korea is a heaven-made foreign kingdom in the east, strategically placed and far away. My intention was not to govern you, so that we can avoid difficulties and live in tranquility. You have requested to become our subject several times, and your expressions have grown firmer. . . . I therefore accept your request, and will treat you equitably, without making any distinction between the civilized and uncivilized. I accept your reverence and sincerity, request that you inherit your former rank, follow your own propriety, and abide by your former laws. . . . [I] have now sent an envoy with a seal to invest you as King of the Koryŏ as before, allowing your rituals and institutions to follow local customs. . . . Serve as our guard on the frontier.[47]

Koryŏ, still reeling from the Mongol onslaught and uncertain which direction Chinese politics were moving in, were only too happy to declare themselves—at least in theory—tributary vassals of the Ming. Meanwhile they kept some links with the Yuan forces still active in Manchuria, a region the Ming armies had yet to reach. One faction at court believed that the changes in China meant an opportunity for Koryŏ to take over areas to the north of the Yalu river that had been under Korean control in the past. As Hongwu gained more information about the situation in and around Korea, he started distrusting Koryŏ officials and berating them for their lack of commitment to the empire. "[You] need to improve your moral excellence and change your behavior in order to protect your country and abandon the stratagem of deception," Emperor Hongwu rebuked the Koryŏ king.[48]

Between 1380 and the early 1390s internal politics in Koryŏ descended into chaos, in part as a result of disagreements on how to handle the country's foreign affairs. The Koryŏ king was murdered and his successor failed to get Ming recognition. Meanwhile different factions at court in Kaesŏng were battling each other. In 1388 the king ordered the leading Korean general, Yi Sŏng-gye, to take his troops across the Yalu and into Manchuria. General Yi tried to argue against the expedition, believing that confronting Ming troops in an area of strategic disadvantage could lead to disaster for Koryŏ. Having been instructed to proceed, General Yi and his forces moved toward the border, but, after a council held at Wihwa Island in the Yalu, the general made the portentous decision to turn back. Moving quickly to take control of the capital, General Yi banished or executed his opponents and forced the king to abdicate. After ruling from behind the throne for four years, Yi Sŏng-gye declared himself king in 1392. He called the new dynasty, and the new state, Chosŏn, meaning "morning freshness." In it was a declaration that Korea, much wanting, would have a new beginning under his rule.[49]

The Ming empire was about revitalization of the Chinese tradition, but also about regulating China's relations with its neighbors. It was a singular project of conquest and cohesion. But Chosŏn was even more of a project. What Yi Sŏng-gye and his advisers did was to build a new state with the intention of remaking Korean society. Their ideological instrument in doing so was neo-Confucianism of the Zhu Xi kind; an uncompromising set of ideals for human behavior, state construction, and social development. Chosŏn intended to structure

31

Korean society according to the moral principles that govern the universe, emphasizing harmony, hierarchy, family, self-cultivation, and learning. It proclaimed righteousness as its key slogan. Chosŏn became an ideologically driven kingdom that sometimes tended toward dogmatism, especially when it highlighted social discipline and state veneration.

In the late fourteenth century much of this still lay in the future. Yi Sŏng-gye, known to posterity as King T'aejo, had to solidify his new dynasty—the first such change in Korea for 500 years—by incorporating old elites and integrating the different parts of the country under Chosŏn rule. For T'aejo and his successors neo-Confucianism was the banner under which the entrenchment of their rule took place. Ideologues such as Chŏng To-jŏn, the main author of the new ruler's legal and administrative codes, emphasized the new beginning on the road to righteousness that the founding of Chosŏn implied. But T'aejo's advisers also stressed the king's own responsibilities: "A ruler's position must be maintained through virtue, so as to gain the people's heart."[50] "On the whole, the ruler relies on the nation, and the nation on its people. The people are the foundation of the nation, of Heaven, and of the ruler. . . . The people are weak but cannot be threatened by might, and they are foolish but cannot be fooled by cleverness."[51] Chosŏn was legitimate and powerful, in other words, only as long as its rulers were virtuous and served the people by upholding Confucian righteousness.

While proclaiming Confucian virtue, the king himself was also busy striking the thousands of little and big compromises with established power-holders that were needed to solidify the new state. Most old families were able to put some of their mem-

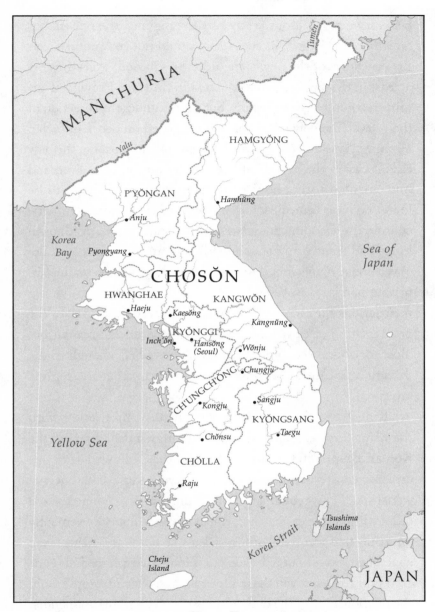

MANCHURIA

Yalu

Tumen

HAMGYŎNG

P'YŎNGAN

•Hamhŭng

•Anju

Korea
Bay

Pyongyang•

CHOSŎN

Sea of
Japan

HWANGHAE

KANGWŎN

•Haeju

•Kaesŏng

Kangnŭng•

KYŎNGGI

Inch'ŏn•

•Hansŏng
(Seoul)

•Wŏnju

CHUNGCH'ŎNG

•Chungju

•Kongju

•Sangju

KYŎNGSANG

Yellow Sea

•Chŏnsu

•Taegu

CHŎLLA

•Raju

Tsushima
Islands

Korea Strait

Cheju
Island

JAPAN

MAP 1.1 Chosŏn Korea, c. 1650

bers into new positions created by the regime. The one matter on which T'aejo and his successors would not compromise was the centrality of the new state order. In Chosŏn, everything—at least in theory—was subordinated to the state. Provincial administrations were important, but served under the direction of the center. The new education system, based on neo-Confucian teachings, was designed in Seoul, then called Hansŏng, the new capital city in the middle of the country on the Han river, and implemented throughout Korea. But compromise had to be found even on some of Chosŏn's key concerns, such as in agriculture, the economic foundation of the state. The early Chosŏn kings had wanted to confiscate all land and re-tenure it under government ownership, but, in reality, most land remained in private hands, even though the state involved itself in issuing instructions for increasing production. Overall, in spite of the proclamation of early Chosŏn as a neo-Confucian revolution, most social and economic changes were gradual, though in the direction of centralization and state-control that the regime professed.[52]

King T'aejo also had to attempt to regulate his relations with the Ming. From Nanjing, Emperor Hongwu had observed the Korean coup d'etat and the changes that followed with increasing consternation and alarm. Koryŏ, after all, had been a vassal state. How could any Korean unilaterally change the old order without the express agreement of the Ming? Conveniently omitting that the "old" order, at least as far as the Ming were concerned, was about a decade old, Hongwu expressed his concern and dismay over these repeated breaches of propriety in the relationship. In the end, taking the advice of his councilors, the emperor relented and grudgingly agreed to de facto accept the new state of affairs in Korea, in part because doing otherwise would have meant war. The Hongwu emperor was far too preoccupied establishing his own dynasty and waging war in the north and west to take such a risk. Instead he wrote directly to T'aejo, saying that

> All peoples under heaven are my loyal sons. I will demonstrate the key to disaster or fortune and allow you to make a fresh start. . . . I will allow you to improve your own reputation and cultivation and then show that I hold you in esteem. If you violate the Way of Heaven again, then you should not regret the punishment that will fall on you.[53]

While still striving to set right his relations with the Ming and with a fierce power struggle among his sons already under way, King T'aejo, exhausted and depressed, abdicated from the throne in 1398. His abdication set off a period of confusion in Chosŏn politics, lasting until his fifth son, Yi Pang-wŏn, was enthroned as King T'aejong in 1400. Even if Ming leaders appeared to look at Korea's unruly politics with horror, Chosŏn elites stubbornly stuck to the concept of linking their new state as closely as possible to China, at least in ideological terms.

Through the political disturbances of the early Chosŏn era there gradually emerged a new administrative and social order. In this process, it suited Chosŏn elites well to appeal to patterns set by an ideal "China," of which very few Koreans had any direct knowledge. Chosŏn kings began referring to their relationship with the Ming as "serving the great" (*sadae* in Korean), especially, of course, when a favor was needed from the Ming court, but also to legitimize what Chosŏn leaders wanted to do in Korea. The quote is from Mengzi, a Confucian text from the fourth century BC, which says that "it requires a wise prince to be able, with a small country, to serve a large one. . . . [He] stands in awe of Heaven. . . . He who stands in awe of Heaven, will protect his own kingdom."[54] "Serving the Great" was a way of protecting Korea from Ming interference and from external enemies. But it was also a way of giving significance to the Chosŏn regime by portraying it as a uniquely close associate of the most powerful state around. And early Ming China's many challenges, domestic and foreign, made it easier for the emperors to accept Chosŏn panegyrics and more difficult to intervene effectively in Korean politics.

But the pragmatic needs of the regime should not get in the way of understanding the ideological single-mindedness of early Chosŏn. The ruling elite firmly believed in the applicability of neo-Confucian doctrines to Korean society. In fact, much of the elite seemed intent to root out other belief systems. Their emphasis on societal cohesion and hierarchical organization was driven by a genuine conviction about the universal applicability of neo-Confucian thinking. For Korea, it was a top-down neo-Confucian revolution, in which Chosŏn elites attempted to implement systems of social ethics alongside changes in administration, education, and military affairs. The purpose was to use Confucian principles to improve society through banishing bad practices and encouraging good behavior at all levels, from the king to peasants in the fields. As the influence of experts on neo-Confucian theory and practice—often referred to as literati—

increased at court, their cudgels of disapprobation could be aimed even at leading officials, whom they suspected of persisting in bad habits of old. As the Chosŏn state developed in the fifteenth and sixteenth centuries, the literati's emphasis on three ways of promoting Confucian virtue—education, supervision, and ritual—became ever more prominent in Korea. The processes created a society that was given to a degree of moral strictness and inflexibility, but also one that was remarkably cohesive, strong, and durable.

At the core of Korea's neo-Confucian project lay clear and specific sets of definitions of social interrelationships. A key one was often referred to as the three primary social bonds. The bonds were between father and son, ruler and subject, and husband and wife. These were hierarchical and based on a set of obligations at both ends of the hierarchy: Obedience, for instance, for sons, subjects, and wives; protection and care for fathers, rulers, and husbands. In this sense Chosŏn ideals were similar to older forms of Confucian thinking. But in Chosŏn Korea these bonds were developed into well-defined relationships among almost all members of society, based on language, rituals, and forms of behavior. Of course these attempts at social micro-management did not always work out, as demonstrated by many occasions of political conflict and confusion in the early Chosŏn era. But over time a very large number of Koreans internalized them and found ways of turning them to their own favor within a regulated society and a well-practiced state.[55]

The neo-Confucian revolution during Korea's fifteenth century was not dissimilar to what was happening at the same time in Ming China, only deeper and longer-lasting. The fact that the two states both revered Confucian principles tied them together, and Chosŏn's *sadae* policy established a relationship that was often expressed in father-son terms, or, at least, older brother-younger brother. Chosŏn attempted, with various degrees of success, to mobilize Ming support in regulating its relations with the Jurchen north of the border and with the Japanese, an increasing seaborne presence in Korean waters. Still, both of these Chosŏn "foreign relations" were complex in terms of its vassal relationship with Ming China. For all of the fifteenth century, the Chosŏn state also rivaled with the Ming for influence among the Jurchen and other groups as yet beyond the reach of the Ming. When the Yongle emperor (1402–1424) tried to regulate the border areas through incorporating all the various regions the Ming laid claim to directly into the empire, the Koreans became increasingly concerned. The Chosŏn king told his court: "The emperor likes doing grandiose things to impress people. If our country has a little lack of the propriety of serving the great, [he] will send a punitive expedition against us. I believe the most urgent tasks now are, first, to serve him with utmost integrity and, second, to strengthen our fortifications and store our supplies."[56] Yongle's naval expeditions to the west and his attempts at ruling Vietnam as a Ming province convinced Chosŏn that the Chinese might act against them, too. But Chosŏn involvement north of the border did not cease; Korean leaders seemed to have thought that helping create a buffer zone inside the empire would improve their overall security.

The enthronement of the Yongle emperor meant the stabilization of the Ming state after years of political unrest and civil wars. Having grabbed the throne from his nephew through conquest, Yongle embarked on a set of massive projects to develop China's economy and its foreign power. The seaborne voyages of exploration to the west, commanded by his Muslim admiral Zheng He, for a time extended the Ming's naval reach to the Indian ocean. In southeast and central Asia, Yongle's foreign policy was relentlessly expansionist, driven in part by the emperor's obsession with obedience and submission, which some historians portray as originating in the dubious circumstances of Yongle's own elevation. Even though the naval expeditions would be largely discontinued after 1450 and the Ming's regional enemies began transforming their own military capabilities to better resist pressure from the empire, the Yongle era set many patterns for how the Ming would attempt to organize its relations with other states. At its core lay claims to a unique universality of the Ming empire and its emperor, at least within a regional context. For more than 200 years, the Ming elite fought hard to preserve this claim against all who opposed it, including at times of great adversity, such as when their emperor Zhengtong was taken prisoner in 1449 in a botched attempt at defeating the western Mongols. But even such a disaster did not dent Ming exceptionalism. Proclaiming Zhengtong's brother as the new emperor, Ming leaders immediately issued an uncompromising prescript, asserting the responsibility of the Ming empire for the welfare of the whole world.[57]

Throughout the Ming era, China-Korean relations incorporated a number of themes: Security, territory, and sovereignty, as well as exchanges of goods, ideas, and technology. From Yongle's time onward, the relationship stabilized, as successive generations of Chosŏn leaders became convinced that Ming

emperors, in spite of their outward power, did not intend to colonize Korea. The strongest guarantee against such an attack by its powerful neighbor, Koreans felt, was strict adherence to established rituals in all forms of interactions with the Chinese. The content of these rituals was important. Terms and phrases all came out of past precedent and, if possible, from

MAP 1.2 Ming Empire, c. 1520

the core Confucian corpus. *Where* the interaction took place was essential, not least because of the performative qualities of the encounters. In times of tension, the expression and performance of ritual at the imperial court in Beijing took on a particular significance.[58] The implied meaning of this ritual intercourse was always the same: The Ming were the older brother

41

of the Chosŏn. The rights and obligations that existed between older and younger brothers in the Confucian rulebook also went for the relationship between the two states. The younger brother should respect and obey the older, come to his aid when needed, and laud his qualities to all others. The older brother should protect and enlighten the younger, represent him toward others, and treat him with care and forgiveness. Together the brothers should conserve and extend the family's wealth, prestige, and position.

This relationship was, at least in form, continued through the Ming and Qing eras, and right up to the late nineteenth century. The resolution of a clash in 1864 when Koreans had taken timber on the Qing side of the border can serve as an example. The Chosŏn king apologized, and the Qing Emperor promised to supply the timber the Koreans needed. King Kojong memorialized:

> I am frightened and ashamed, and there is no way I can be forgiven. Indeed, the Imperial Sagely Grace is broad and vast, greater than any river or sea. I never imagined I would escape blame and punishment, yet Permission has been granted to supply timber. With the command to dispatch men to receive it, I am emotionally overcome in the extreme and rendered utterly speechless. With all due reverence, I will send men to receive the timber. The subjects of our entire country exhaustively sing the praises of the Imperial Virtue of caring for the small and cherishing those from afar, surpassing all that has come before.[59]

Some of the ritual relationship between China and Korea in the Ming era was organized through tribute missions.[60] Usually the Chosŏn kings sent three congratulatory missions to Beijing each year, one at New Year and one at the birthdays of the emperor and the heir apparent. But in addition there were sometimes missions at winter solstice or missions of thanks, condolences, cherishing virtue, presenting horses, or simply celebrating the emperor's sagacity. All of these missions carried tribute for the emperor: Gold and other precious metals or stones, leopard or sea-otter skins, tea, ginseng, grain, or people—slaves, young girls, and eunuchs. At times the Chinese presented formal requests, but most often the Koreans knew what the other side wanted and supplied their missions accordingly. In fact, it was often the Korean kings who pushed for more tribute missions, in order to cement their relations with the Ming. Over time, the contact between the two sides led to an intermingling of Ming ceremonials and rituals with Korean traditions in Chosŏn. By the late sixteenth century, Korean ritual practices had become strongly influenced by those north of the border, in spite of many Chosŏn scholars insistence that Korean practices were as good, if not superior, to Chinese.

An example may help us understand the relationship with regard to tribute.[61] In 1524 the Jiajing emperor, who had inherited the throne from his uncle, decided to elevate his father and mother to imperial status. The king immediately decided to send a congratulatory mission. Most of the Confucian scholars at the Korean court demurred. They saw the emperor's decision as out of tune with Confucian principles. But the king persisted, arguing that when a small state serves a big state, it should not quarrel with the suzerain's definitions of correctness. The king got what he wanted. When learning that Jiajing had been pleased by the arrival of the Korean envoys, the Chosŏn king Chungjong decided that he would send another mission, this time to offer tribute to the emperor in gratitude for his gracious reception of the first mission. And so on it went, except when the Chinese side at times indicated that Chosŏn should temper its willingness to offer tribute. Some Ming officials were concerned both with the expenditure for hosting large groups of Koreans and the suspicion that the visitors made use of their time in Beijing for less savory purposes than offering gifts to the emperor.

The purposes the Chinese officials had in mind were personal enjoyment, intelligence gathering, and first and foremost trade.[62] As soon as the Korean envoys arrived in Beijing, they were met by Chinese merchants who offered good prices for any surplus goods, especially ginseng and furs. Participating in this trade made some Koreans (and Chinese, too) quite wealthy, and for some it was a triple blessing, since they could trade both in Beijing and in Seoul, when Koreans envoys returned and Chinese envoys arrived, as well as along the routes the missions traveled through. It is impossible to estimate the value of this tribute-trade, but given the amount of goods overall and the frequency of the missions, it must have been quite considerable. In the 200 years after 1368, at least 611 major missions traveled from Korea to Beijing, plus a number of lower-level missions, plus missions to Liaoning province on the Korean border. Officials and merchants on both sides could make a good living out of this trade, and it was in their interest to protect and expand it, in spite of government disapproval. Especially in Korea, some leading families referred to it as "our trade," indicating that it played a central role in family finances.

But ideas traveled as well as goods. For Korean emissaries, a major investment in Beijing were Chinese books that could be brought back home. Everything from commentaries on the Confucian classics, to technical manuals and erotic literature was freighted back, copied, reprinted, and sold at high prices to curious Korean buyers. A late sixteenth-century Beijing scholar noted that "People from Chosŏn really like books. The number of their envoys is limited to fifty, but even in the early morning they are out visiting book markets, copying down titles, and asking whomever they meet [about books]. They do not spare money to buy books they do not own, whether an old classic, a new book, or a popular novel."[63] Such exchanges spread Ming knowledge of the world, of agriculture, or hydraulics to Korea and, often, from there to Japan. They also gave rise to personal contacts between Korean and Chinese scholars, links that often lasted a lifetime. Of course not all of this went in one direction. Chinese officials who visited Korea collected Korean books, too, or Chinese books that were difficult to get at home.[64] Though Chosŏn kings tried to limit access to "Chinese information," which sometimes threatened the regime's monopoly on news and knowledge, the exchange of ideas between China and Korea was often as important as official contacts.

Throughout the Ming and Qing eras, imperial envoys to Seoul were subject to multiple restrictions on what they could do and see. It was important to the Chosŏn leaders that Chinese ambassadors did not learn too much about their country or made too many contacts besides those provided for them by officialdom. Korean kings also feared the influence and direction that heterodox views from China could provide for disgruntled inhabitants of Chosŏn, who sometimes chafed under the absolutist ambitions of the state. Not surprisingly, they feared imperial intelligence gathering providing information that could be turned against Chosŏn in a crisis. While Chosŏn agents seem to have been quite successful in Beijing and elsewhere in the empire, imperial representatives struggled to get the information they wanted on the Korean side, even when the envoys were ethnic Koreans, born inside the empire or eunuchs sent as tribute long ago. The early modern China-Korea relationship had many facets, and among the most important were information and intelligence.[65]

In the sixteenth century, one aspect of international affairs that Koreans were observing much more closely than Chinese was the rise of alternative powers in the region. For centuries, the Japanese had been derided by officials in the empire and Korea alike as eastern barbarians beyond the sea (and, implicitly, beyond the realm of civilization). In reality Japan was rapidly strengthening, in part through ideas and practices that had been imported from China and Korea. Politically Japan was divided, to the point that several leaders in the fifteenth century tried to improve their relative position by seeking vassalage under the Ming empire. The Ming were lukewarm to these proposals, both because of the confused state of Japanese politics and because there was disagreement at court about whether the Japanese had the necessary level of civilization for a tributary relationship to make sense. Meanwhile the Koreans suffered under increasing numbers of Japanese pirate attacks along their coasts, routinely reporting to Beijing to inform the emperor about the ferocity of the sea-dwelling barbarians.

In the 1570s and '80s the battle for power among Japan's leading clans intensified, with the surprising result that one daimyo (feudal lord) in the end was able to unify all of the country under his rule. This was Toyotomi Hideyoshi, who ruled as shogun from 1586 to 1598. Hideyoshi, as he is generally known, saw himself not only as the great unifier of Japan but also as chosen to become a world conqueror. Gradually he developed a plan for attacking the Ming empire through Korea. Before the unification of Japan was complete, Hideyoshi said that he had "sent fast ships in order to urge even Korea to pay homage to the Japanese emperor, stating that, if it does not, I shall conquer it next year. I shall take even China in hand, and have control of it during my lifetime." He told his generals: "It is not Ming China alone that is destined to be subjugated by us, but India, the Philippines, and many islands in the South Sea will share a like fate. We are now occupying the most conspicuous and enviable position in the world."[66]

But it was not only in Japan that a rival to the Ming-centered international system in eastern Asia seemed to be emerging in the late sixteenth century. The Jurchen, a set of Tungusic-speaking groups with origins in eastern Siberia, had once formed a mighty state in northern China, Manchuria, and the Pacific coast. When this Jin state had been conquered by the Mongols in the thirteenth century, the Jurchen groups dispersed, but they kept a strong hold on territories immediately north of the Korean border. In the 1580s a chief named Nurhaci began uniting the Jurchen under his banner. By the early 1600s Nurhaci's state had grown powerful, attracting Chinese, Mongols, and Koreans to its banners, tempted in part by the spoils of conquest and in part by its leader's condemnation of Ming abuses and corruption. In 1616 Nurhaci declared the Jin resurrected, and two decades later his son and successor Hongtaiji changed the name of his people to the Manchu and his state to the Qing empire. It was an open declaration of war against the Ming by what had begun as a ragtag band of warriors in the northern wastes.

The Japanese and the Manchu were to upend the stable order that had ruled eastern Asia for more than 200 years. As often happened, before or after, the Koreans got caught in the middle of these epochal transformations of power. In 1590 Hideyoshi sent another letter to the Korean king, informing the sovereign that he wanted to "introduce Japanese customs and values to the 400 and more provinces of that country [China] and bestow upon it the benefits of [Japanese] imperial rule and culture of the coming hundred million years."[67] The shogun's proclamation seemed preposterous. Japan had just come out of a period of disunity and warfare, and it was hard to believe that the country could be an example for anyone. But the vision of greatness was not, in itself, more absurd than the Ming or Chosŏn projects had been at their inception. The distances over which Japan's dominion would be projected were immense, though, and Hideyoshi's lack of measure equally vast. He had taken from the Ming the idea of universal rule, but had not had the time to temper it with gradualism and compromises of the Hongwu or T'aejo kind.[68]

Hideyoshi was soundly derided for his ambition by the Korean king, who declared his eternal loyalty to the empire. King Sŏnjo wrote to the Japanese shogun,

As for our kingdom, generation after generation, we have reverently adhered and attended to all duties and obligations due from a tributary state of [China]. In fact, [China] has always regarded our kingdom as a part of its own nation. Our two nations have already kept each other informed of all national events and affairs. Each has given ready assistance when the other has suffered calamity or has been in trouble. Our two nations have acted as a single family, maintaining the relationship of father and son as well as that of ruler and subject. . . . We shall certainly not desert 'our lord and father nation' [China] and join with a neighboring nation in her unjust and unwise military undertaking. . . . We shall certainly not take up arms against the supreme nation.[69]

Hideyoshi began his invasion on May 23, 1592. An army of almost 20,000 men landed in southeastern Korea and surrounded the port city of Busan, a place well known to Japanese merchants. Korean resistance crumbled almost immediately. We do not know how many Koreans were killed at Busan, but the number must have been in the thousands. In nearby Tongnae, which Hideyoshi's forces reached the next day, 3,000 people were beheaded and 500 taken as prisoners of war. Japanese soldiers, having just emerged from a brutal civil war, had been ordered to show no mercy. Their commanders wanted fear and confusion to spread among Koreans across the peninsula, making it easier for the Japanese to reach Ming China, their real target in the war.

Having been at peace for 200 years, Chosŏn was poorly prepared for war. In town after town, garrison after garrison, the ill-equipped and ill-trained Korean forces were routed by the Japanese. In addition to superior organization, the Japanese soldiers had access to better weapons, including arquebuses and breech-loading canons, and swords and arrows of better quality. There were widespread Japanese atrocities against the civilian population, sometimes because the Koreans did not cooperate with the invaders but more often because they simply got in the way of the advancing troops. On June 11 the Japanese entered the capital, Seoul, unopposed. The Chosŏn king and court had fled north. The same pattern repeated itself at Kaesŏng and Pyongyang. In some places chaos and lawlessness broke out well before the arrival of the Japanese troops, because Chosŏn authority had collapsed when its administrators ran away. Watching the advance of his troops from Japan, Hideyoshi began thinking about relocating the Japanese emperor to Beijing, as titular head of a new east Asian empire under his leadership.[70]

But there were two challenges rising to Hideyoshi's ambition. One was the fury of ordinary Koreans against the violence that had been unleashed against them. The other was the Ming empire, which slowly was getting its act together to defend its tributary. While it had been reasonably clear in Beijing all along that the Ming had to send troops to Korea, the question was when and how. The Wanli emperor was already engaged in suppressing a rebellion in the west, and dealing with restive Mongols in the north. Although he had already sent local troops from Liaodong to assist the Koreans in the summer of 1592, the emperor did not want to commit major forces to Korea before he absolutely had to. He promised pivotal aid to the Koreans:[71]

The Emperor decrees to the king of Chosŏn as follows. Your country has for generations guarded the eastern periphery and served [us] with consummate propriety. Rituals and decorum, culture, and economy have prospered and so it was called a paradise. We learned recently that Dwarf Slaves have consolidated and invaded [your country]. They assaulted and captured the capital and attacked and occupied Pyongyang. The people are in chaos and misery; disorder prevails far and wide; the king has taken refuge on the western sea coast and is reduced to holding court in the wilderness. When we think that national territory has been taken away from you, and you are plunged into confusion, our heart is also deeply saddened. We have heard the urgent news and have already decreed to the officials in charge of outlying areas to assemble troops and to carry out a rescue mission.[72]

In the autumn of 1592 it started becoming clear to Wanli's advisers that the Japanese offensive was not just an escapade by mercurial island dwellers. It was a concrete and immediate danger to the northeastern parts of the empire. One of Wanli's advisers memorialized:

Korea lies under our shoulder to the east. Pyongyang is adjacent to the Yalu River. . . . If Japan takes over Korea and trains Koreans as soldiers under its command, while taking

51

military supplies from Korea to build a powerful army against us, this could . . . cut off our food supplies, while conquering Liaodong from Korea's Chŏlla and Kyŏngsang provinces. . . . Beijing will then be in a difficult position. This is a security concern for us.[73]

The Ming mobilized some of their central armies in the winter of 1592 and joined them with forces already in the northeast. In January 1593 they crossed into Korea. Pyongyang was reconquered by allied Ming and Chosŏn forces on February 8. The Japanese had been unprepared for the counterattack and were driven rapidly toward the south, with great losses. More than 7,000 Japanese soldiers fell just in the Pyongyang offensive. Castigated by a furious Hideyoshi, the invaders tried to make a stand in central Korea, north of the capital. But here they ran into the other major challenge to their power. Ever since the first chaotic weeks after the invasion, groups of Korean irregulars had been mobilizing independently of the Chosŏn state. The desperate King Sŏnjo had urged all Koreans to take up arms and defend the country. By late autumn some of these guerrilla groups, sometimes referring to themselves as the Righteous Army, had begun inflicting some damage on the Japanese, who in turn took terrible revenge on the civilian population. Letters went around—for the first time using Korean script for official purposes, in part so that the Japanese could not easily read them—stressing the duty of ordinary Koreans to fight the enemy, even if the state had not succeeded in resisting. "Ultimately," the historian Haboush says about these letters, they were "a contemplation on personal and collective identity—on the meaning of living and dying as moral human beings, and of remaining Korean and not be transformed into a 'bestial' other."[74] In spite of the state's failure in war, generations of schooling in Neo-Confucian values had a critical effect.

In her seminal book on the war, which the Koreans call the Imjin War after the calendar name for the year in which it started, Haboush argues that the Japanese attack and the events that followed confirmed the Korean concept of nation. She identifies seven themes in this concept that would have a lasting effect: the experience of Japanese atrocities, the reverence for ancestral lands, the identification of Korean culture, the sense of moral duty, the need to sacrifice, the defense of civilization, and the reverence for peace and order. To these could be added an increased sense of a special status with regard to the Chinese center of civilization and a profound feeling of victimhood and fragility. The Righteous Army fit right into this framework, even though ordinary Koreans, who fought and died for their homes and families, probably would have put it in simpler and more straightforward terms. But even to them the idea of righteousness—of a just cause combined with Korean virtues— stood at the center. They used it to recruit, organize, and fight in ways that their opponents found increasingly deadly.

By late spring of 1593 it had become abundantly clear to the Japanese that no quick victory was in sight, and that the aim of conquering the Ming empire was beyond reach. The war bogged down into isolated battles, where the Japanese usually won when they could concentrate their forces but were vulnerable when detachments were isolated and assailed. Along the coast the Japanese navy repeatedly lost out to Korean vessels, which had the advantage of better commanders with local knowledge who could use the superior maneuverability of the smaller Korean ships. The Korean naval commanders, such as the fabled Yi Sun-sin, quickly learned how to use artillery that they had taken from the enemy or obtained from the Chinese. The so-called turtle-ships, which did much damage to the enemy, combined these assets with strong defenses—heavy planks and sharp spikes shielded the Korean sailors from their ships being boarded. The Japanese commanders agreed to peace talks with the Ming, which dragged out for several years, with the Koreans more or less excluded from the process.

Chosŏn's relations with the Ming during the war were complex for both sides. The Koreans were very aware that their state depended on Ming support for survival, even though the Koreans did much of the fighting. But they also resented what they regarded as excessive Ming demands for supplies for the imperial troops, the routine abuse of Korean civilians, and Ming attempts to dictate military strategies. The Koreans' biggest fear was that the Ming would negotiate some peace arrangement with Hideyoshi over their heads, ceding Korean territory in the bargain. As for the Chinese, they often derided what they perceived as Korean weakness, disorganization, and cowardice. Beijing suspected that some Chosŏn officials, governors, and generals had made secret contact with the Japanese. A few Ming counselors recommended that the Chosŏn king be forced to abdicate and that Korea be incorporated into the empire.[75] Even though the Wanli emperor reacted strongly against these suggestions as improper in terms of a Confucian sense of obligation, he was keenly aware of the empire's expenditures in supporting Chosŏn. Put together with other military outlay in the west and in the north, and not least in the northeast, where the Ming struggled to contain Jurchen exploits, the war forced the emperor to raise taxes in ways that the Ming had always tried to avoid.

After almost two years of stumbling peace negotiations, the war reignited in 1597, with renewed Japanese attacks against Korea. Hideyoshi had believed he could at least get the Ming to recognize him as an equal. But the Ming negotiators, who had traveled to Japan, had simply offered him the chance to be accepted as a vassal of the empire, with all the rights and obligations that went with such a status. Furious, the Japanese shogun unleashed another wave of seaborne invasion forces, this time numbering around 150,000. The Ming responded by sending large forces of their own into Korea. This time the emperor was determined not to be caught unaware of Japanese aggression. The result was as much of a stalemate as the first time around, but with Korean civilian casualties being even worse, because both of the foreign armies attempted to force locals to work for them and feed them. Then, on September 18, 1598, Hideyoshi died. His successors immediately decided to withdraw from Korea, but before they managed to do so, Chosŏn and Ming naval forces had attacked and destroyed half of the Japanese fleet off the coast of Namhae Island. The war had turned into a disaster for Japan, but Korea had suffered the worst consequences.

The Chosŏn court mourned the Korean losses. But for them what mattered most was that the Chosŏn regime itself had pulled through. The Chosŏn king, Sŏnjo, had survived politically by tying himself ever closer to the Ming. For most elite Koreans, he was the one who—by his personal qualities, loyalty, and, not least, righteousness—had delivered Ming intervention and thereby saved Korea. But Sŏnjo himself and his closest advisors knew that the truth was more complicated. There had been much tension between Ming and Chosŏn officials during the war, not least on military matters. Sŏnjo had learned the hard way that ideological cohesion with the Ming, which he profoundly believed in, was not enough to save his state. He had had to make practical concessions and incessantly convince his Chinese interlocutors of Korea's subservience and obedience. Out of the ordeal came two principles that Sŏnjo passed on to his heirs: that the Ming had shown their greatness by saving Chosŏn from Japan, and that none but Koreans could be trusted to uphold the interests of the state and the country. The two lessons could easily go together as long as the relative significance of each was calibrated according to the situation Korea at any time found itself in, domestically and internationally. And Sŏnjo's successors would soon need to apply them under difficult circumstances.

Just as the Japanese were evacuating the peninsula and returning across the sea, more trouble was brewing north of the border. As the Jurchen state expanded and metamorphosed into a hybrid entity that was Manchurian, Central Asian, and Chinese all in one, Chosŏn leaders sensed that further disorder was coming. They were well informed about happenings within the state that now again called itself Jin; some Koreans had joined Nurhaci's project voluntarily, but more were just caught up in the turmoil created by the Jurchen encroachments. A few were sending information to Chosŏn. The picture the Korean spies painted was of a massive force in the making, with pretensions of ruling all of China, and perhaps Korea too. Chosŏn fears were confirmed in May 1618 when Nurhaci sent a letter to the new Korean king proclaiming that he had rebelled against the Ming and warning Chosŏn not to aid his enemies.

The debate that followed at the Chosŏn court was intense and furious. Korea had been left devastated by the wars against Japan twenty years earlier and had not yet recovered. Some ministers therefore argued that Chosŏn should stay out of Nurhaci's conflict with the Ming. But the majority, including the king, argued for carefully calibrated assistance to the Ming. Chosŏn owed the empire a debt of gratitude for helping to defeat Hideyoshi. Also, Nurhaci's audacious troops were a threat to Korea that could be defeated only by allying with the Ming. Most officials still believed that the Ming would ultimately win the contest for China. But the most important argument for supporting the emperor was that it was simply the right thing to do: Chosŏn was a Ming vassal. As long as the emperor held the mandate of heaven, Chosŏn's loyalty was to him.

Korean troops entered China in February 1619 after having been ordered to do so by the Ming emperor. Two months later they and the Ming's northern armies confronted Nurhaci's troops at Sarhu, some 400 miles from Beijing. They outnumbered the Jurchen's forces by two to one, and they lost everything. Nurhaci's men were well trained, well integrated, and vigorous, led by officers who were driven by righteous grievance and the prospect of rich loot. The Chinese and Korean forces had nothing to match. They were in the field because their monarchs had ordered them there. As the rebels pressed their attack, Ming resistance collapsed. The imperial forces lost perhaps 50,000 men, ten times the casualties of their opponents. It was clear that the balance of power was shifting in Northeast Asia. Chosŏn was more exposed than ever before.

The Chosŏn king, still known as Prince Kwanghae because the Ming had objected to his succession, now faced a terrible choice. All his political and military insights told him that if Korea continued to refuse to have dealings with the Jurchens, disaster would ensue. But his Confucian instincts told him to stay loyal to the emperor and to the Ming. With intense factional strife raging at court, the king started a carefully crafted exchange of letters with Nurhaci. But as the tide of war turned further to his advantage in China, the Jurchen leader had little reason to compromise with Chosŏn. Nurhaci insisted on a treaty that recognized the Jin as an empire equal to the Ming. Having gotten wind of Chosŏn contacts with their enemies, Ming leaders threatened to send a governor-general to rule Chosŏn. The Koreans were disgraceful, one Ming commander said, like "a rat looking both ways."[76] As factional infighting in Chosŏn crescendoed, officials and officers from a loyalist group carried out a coup d'état in 1623, removing Prince Kwanghae and replacing him with his twenty-eight-year-old nephew, known as King Injo.

With a group of ultraloyalists in command and an inexperienced king on the throne, Chosŏn slid toward disaster. As factions continued to battle each other over control of the Chosŏn state, one of Nurhaci's most experienced armies was sent to invade Korea in 1627. Pyongyang fell quickly, and the Jurchen-led troops advanced on Seoul. King Injo fled to Kanghwa Island, from where he negotiated a nonaggression treaty with the invaders, providing them with hostages and promises to abandon Ming titles, style, and calendars. If Nurhaci had not died as the invasion was being prepared, the Koreans would probably have fared far worse. His son and successor, known as Hongtaiji, was at first more preoccupied with getting ready for a full-scale invasion of China through stockpiling resources and military equipment as well as probing Ming defenses in the northeast. He also prepared a new ideological framework for his rule. In 1635 he renamed his people the Manchus, and the following year he declared a new empire, Qing, meaning "luminous" or "clear," with himself as the Sublime Virtue (*Chongde*) emperor.

In spite of the threat of severe consequences, the Chosŏn elite refused to follow the new empire's dictate that it should break all contact with the Ming. On the contrary, as Manchu armies descended on China, King Injo, in part responding to pressure from Korean loyalists, became more vocal in his support for the beleaguered empire. He refused to receive the Qing ambassadors carrying Hongtaiji's letters, and he drove the envoys out of Seoul as the populace shouted "barbarians" and "fools" at them. With the help of his most learned neo-Confucian advisers, he then composed an intransigent edict of noncooperation. Ordering the letters the ambassadors had left behind to be burned, King Injo proclaimed that he had to uphold the principle of righteousness even against the threat of a catastrophe to his state and its people. His country had always revered and served the Ming, and would not rebel. Chosŏn, the king admitted, was neither rich nor powerful. But what the country possessed was Confucian righteousness, and it would not give that up when threatened by barbarians.[77]

The Qing punishment was swift. In December 1636 Hongtaiji's troops attacked Korea, overrunning the north and occupying the capital. The king fled to the mountains, where he and his retinue were quickly surrounded by the invading forces. Qing commanders offered talks. King Injo hesitated. He performed the rituals to celebrate the Ming emperor's birthday, bowing deeply in the direction of Beijing. Then he sent officials to negotiate with the Qing. This time Hongtaiji, having arrived in Korea himself to oversee the invasion, demanded full and immediate submission. When Injo and the Chosŏn court tried to get away with limited arrangements, like a decade earlier, the Qing troops shelled the fortress where the king had taken refuge. King Injo chose surrender over death. On February 24, 1637, he walked up to a great throne that the invaders had built at Samjŏn-do and prostrated himself three times before Hongtaiji, handing over for destruction the imperial seal issued by the Ming, and swearing to serve loyally as a vassal to the new empire. The Ming era in Korea was over. Hereafter everything, from calendars to foreign policies, had to be set by the standards of the Qing. But, against the odds, Chosŏn had yet again survived as a self-governing polity.

Given the huge disparity in power, it is reasonable to ask why the Qing did not simply incorporate Chosŏn fully into their expanding empire.[78] There seem to have been two main reasons. One was that the Manchus and their allies were preoccupied with the much more important all-out war against the Ming. Chosŏn had been forced to submit and had, so it claimed, given up on assisting the enemies of the Qing. Hongtaiji had bigger fish to fry and was wise enough to leave well enough alone on the Korean Peninsula. But Chosŏn's survival was also assisted by set precedent. The Qing wanted to replace the Ming. They wanted to become the empire instead of the empire that existed. Some scholars say that they wanted to become China, while also continuing to be more than China elsewhere. In order to do so, they had to conform to most of the precedents set by the Ming, while attempting to turn them to their own advantage. This is in many ways how the imperial ideology of the Qing functioned: They were both China and more than China, an empire that centered on the Manchu imperial family and encompassed vast territories, but also a legitimate successor to the Ming and everything that had gone before them, as witnessed by their residence in the Ming imperial city in Beijing after they conquered it in 1644.[79]

The Qing therefore continued to see Korea as an "outer" vassal, even if temptations to incorporate Korea into the empire for practical reasons must at times have run high in Beijing. With some remnants of the Ming regime still at large in southern China, and with Taiwan still ruled by a group loyal to the defeated dynasty, there was a residual fear in the Qing capital that Chosŏn might aid a Ming comeback at some point. When a rebellion broke out against Qing rule in the south in the 1670s, these fears were heightened. But the Qing elite, which included a number of people of Korean descent, was smart enough not to act against Chosŏn as long as the formal requirements for a vassal were kept up by the Korean side. Chosŏn was also lucky that Hongtaiji's son and grandson both inherited the title when they were children, and therefore had time to be socialized into the very special relationship that existed between their empire and Korea. For the emperor Kangxi, Hongtaiji's grandson who ruled China for more than sixty years (1661–1722), these lessons were particularly important, not least because he set the pattern for the empire's foreign relations over the 200 years that followed his reign.

Manchu suspicions about Chosŏn allegiances were very much rooted in Korean realities. King Injo's successor, Hyojong, was a Ming loyalist who—although he performed the necessary rituals of subservience to the Qing—hoped and expected that Ming rule would soon return. In the 1670s, as the Qing faced their first serious rebellion from within, a number of Korean officials urged the king to make common cause with the rebels and send troops to their aid. Although more pragmatic advice of noninterference won the day in Seoul, the attitude toward the Qing did not improve after the young Kangxi emperor put down the rebellion. In 1686 Qing officials forced the Chosŏn king to pay reparations after Korean incursions across the border. In 1704 the Chosŏn authorities, in a direct affront to their suzerain, erected a temple to honor Ming emperors, including Chongzhen, the last Ming monarch, who had committed suicide before the Qing takeover of Beijing. But Kangxi refused to retaliate. To him the position of Chosŏn as a reluctant vassal was good enough, as long as formal proprieties were kept. The emperor knew that making excessive demands against Korea would be futile, unless he was willing to use blunt force to back them up. And Kangxi had learned that there were many worse enemies of his dynasty's rule than the Koreans, both among the Chinese and in Central Asia. Instead of confronting

Chosŏn, he chose to offer it better conditions for its adherence to the empire: reduced tribute, imperial commendations, and more opportunities for trade.

Korean unwillingness to conform to Qing rule in the seventeenth and early eighteenth centuries came out of a deepening sense of cultural superiority among the Chosŏn elite. After the Qing conquest of China, many upper-class Koreans saw themselves as the last vestige of civilization in a region that had been overrun by barbarian rulers. The reversal of roles vis-à-vis China was tortuous but swift. Within less than a generation, China went from being seen as the abode of civilization to being a danger zone of cultural depravity. These labels were applied not only to the Manchus and their allies, but to all Chinese who had permitted the disaster to take place. In contrast, Chosŏn (its surrender to the Qing conveniently disregarded) became the arbiter of Confucian virtue. The label "little China," which Koreans had sometimes bestowed on their own country to signify their proud closeness to the center of civilization, in the mid-seventeenth century became shorthand for "real China," the small state where culture and virtue had miraculously survived.[80] Joining the memory of sacrifice during the Imjin War, the self-ascribed role as guardians of Confucian propriety made a strong argument for Korean distinction as an abode of righteousness in an injurious world.[81]

Inside Chosŏn, the regime's self-image resulted in an increasingly conservative society, in which (to Chinese visitors, at least) customs, writings, and dress seemed frozen in time. The Chosŏn elite, the *yangban* or officials class, attempted to behave as if they were Ming dynasty Confucian scholars. They dressed the part, in costumes that would have been recognizable in China 200 years before. They jealously guarded any kind of information that went out to the people at large; one Chinese visitor observed that one could live a whole life in Korea and not realize that the Ming empire no longer existed and that Chosŏn now was a vassal of the Qing. Meanwhile, the elite's sense of guardianship over all of Korean society deepened. Peasants, tradesmen, young people, and women saw their roles become so curtailed that they had little say over their own lives. The price Korea paid for autonomy and ideological cohesion was, in many ways, a self-contained society, which was more cut off from the rest of region than it had ever been before.[82]

After its consolidation, the Qing empire, Chosŏn's nominal suzerain, became an expansionist power of unrivaled strength in its region. Having subjugated most of Central Asia and Mongolia, as well as parts of the Pacific coast north of Korea, it turned to the Himalayas and Vietnam, with military expeditions against anyone who dared oppose Qing authority. In the midst of this imperialist frenzy, why did the Qing emperors leave Korea alone, in spite of the Chosŏn elite's disdain for the empire's claims to legitimacy? The most important reason was that all emperors after Kangxi recognized that the use of force against Korea would not change anything. They were heartened by the fact that the Chosŏn elite proclaimed belief in exactly the same neo-Confucian ideas and principles that the Qing emperors themselves adhered to. They also had a need for a state that was, in the Qing imaginary, a model vassal, one that adhered to correctness internally and treated Qing with punctilious subservience externally. Koreans knew how to use the correct phrases and forms of behavior toward the Qing. At court in Beijing, during the long rule of Kangxi's grandson, the emperor Qianlong (1735–1796), Chosŏn behavior was often contrasted positively with that of other vassals or even governors of faraway territories within the empire itself. The Manchus and those who served them then hoped that Korean dependence on the Qing would, over time, bend hearts and minds toward the new empire.[83]

In this they were not entirely wrong. By the mid-eighteenth century some Korean scholar-officials had begun chafing under the heavy orthodoxy of the Chosŏn regime. They advocated what they called "practical learning" (*sirhak*) as a supplement to neo-Confucian doctrine. It was not so much that these thinkers tried to move away from Chosŏn's path of heavy reliance on Confucianism. But they wanted to see it enlightened by ideas for organization, welfare, science, and technology that came from outside the Korean experience and, especially, those that came from the Qing empire. In the mid-eighteenth century the Qing was at the height of its power and was itself pulling in ideas and practices from all over the world. Koreans who went on tribute missions to China collected books and met with Qing intellectuals, much as they had done during the Ming. Many of them were left deeply impressed by the changes that were taking place in the empire and dismayed by the conservatism of Chosŏn. In spite of the regime's attempts to regulate all access to such information at home in Korea, the dissemination of new ideas through contact with the empire continued all the way up to the fall of the Chosŏn.[84]

Another link between Qing and Chosŏn that developed in the eighteenth century was trade across the border. Neither state was officially much in favor of trade, but both were willing to accept it if it could be kept within bounds and, preferably, taxed. Some of this trade took place when Chosŏn missions visited Beijing, and, to a smaller degree, when embassies from Qing went to Seoul. But there also grew up a large number of commercialized border stations, which, over time, became conduits for the movement of people and goods. Ginseng, furs, and agricultural products went to China, as did large amounts of silver to pay for Chinese luxury goods imported to Korea: silk, tea, jade, ceramics, books, and art. As the ancestral lands of the Manchu rulers, the Qing's vast Manchurian regions were still kept off-limits to Koreans and Chinese alike. But as soon as that began to change in the nineteenth century, Manchuria exerted a strong attraction for Koreans looking for land and opportunity and, perhaps, an escape from stifling regimentation at home.[85]

During the eighteenth century, Koreans who visited Beijing began to notice new kinds of foreigners who had entered the capital in small numbers from the West. The European presence in Beijing intrigued the Koreans, who sent reports home about the newcomers' behavior and products. Soon European goods also started to make their way to Korea through the missions that came to Beijing. Some Korean envoys started interacting with Russian representatives, out of curiosity more than anything else. Chosŏn authorities attempted to limited such contacts with Russians or other Europeans. They thought liaisons with the "new" foreigners could give rise to trouble with the Qing government or, worse, the spread of heterodox ideas, not least about religion, to Korea—although at first there did not seem to be much chance of the latter, in spite of the Koreans curiosity. One early nineteenth-century Korean visitor to a Christian church reported:

> Upon opening the curtain and entering inside, there is a dead man hanging on the wall opposite. There is a cross-shaped wooden panel on which a man is nailed at the head, legs and arms. It looks like the punishment of tearing a person tied to a cart. The skin of the man is white. His skin, flesh, nails, and hair look real and I can't tell whether the bare body is real or not. Red blood spills out and drips down from the nailed areas, from head to toe. It was as if he had died a few moments ago and his body is still warm. I felt ill and was unable to look at it straight.[86]

As the immediacy of relations between Qing and Chosŏn improved in the latter half of the eighteenth century, the first general contacts between the Qing empire and European countries began. Several British trade and diplomatic missions were sent to Beijing to seek representation and economic privileges, and—though all were turned away by the Qing—it was clear to both Chinese and Koreans that Western presence in East Asian waters would continue. The Korean delegation sent to celebrate the Qianlong emperor's eightieth birthday in 1790 heard about the Western attempts to establish relations with the empire, and the deputation sent to mark Qianlong's abdication in 1795 did pick up news about the British emissary George Macartney's unsuccessful embassy to Beijing two years earlier. In the early nineteenth century, Koreans often attempted to get information about the foreigners from Chinese sources. Britain, one Korean account said, "is located farther away than any other Western country, and is 100,000 li from China by sea. British people are all very quick and fierce and like to loot. Neighboring countries are afraid of her. . . . The land is vast with a large population of people, and it is the strongest country beyond the West. Also, British people are good swimmers and in water they move as swiftly as wild ducks."[87]

The early nineteenth century saw two parallel processes that would affect the relationship between China and Korea over the next hundred years. One was the gradual improvement in connections between the Chosŏn and Qing states. Qianlong's steady but forceful diplomacy, and the long time that was given to him in carrying it out, brought Korean regard for the emperor's person almost back to where it had been in late Ming. By the early nineteenth century many Korean leaders were speaking about the Qing in a form, at least, indistinguishable from what their counterparts had done during the former empire. The other process was the slow encroachment of Western powers on the eastern Asian international system with the Qing at its center. As ships from Britain, France, and the United States started to show up in their waters, Koreans began to reassess their mental maps. "What is commonly called the four seas refers only to China," commented Yi Su-kwang, one of the Korean emissaries to Beijing, "but this is not the four seas of the world."[88]

Given the duality in Korean approaches to China and the wider world that was just becoming visible, it is not surprising that the first clash between the European empires and the Qing empire, what we call the first Opium War, pushed Chosŏn in two different directions at the same time. On the one hand, it did not take long for Chosŏn elites to realize that the Qing had lost its first engagements with Britain and that the empire had looked weak militarily. This made a strong impression in Korea, although the elite were divided on whether this was a temporary setback for the Qing or a more lasting one. On the other hand, the Western appearance did not reduce Chosŏn dependence on the Qing. In a way it increased it. Regardless of their differences in the past, the predominant nineteenth-century Chosŏn elite believed that they and the elites across the border now shared a desire to protect propriety and correctness when faced with domestic heterodoxy and disturbances. The advent of Christianity in Korea, more and more noticeable in the mid-nineteenth century, frightened the Chosŏn elites. Under investigation, a Korean Christian had confessed that "the English people frequently say 'China is a large country but it is unable to oppose us.' Chosŏn is a small country; how can it prohibit Catholicism until the end?"[89] For both Beijing and Seoul, dissension and idolatry seemed to lurk around the corner.

The first encounters with Western imperial power, therefore, did not drive Qing and Chosŏn apart. If anything, it drove them closer together. The sense of an accepted world order being under threat was maximized by social changes that were taking place inside both countries. Increasing commercial activity transported new ideas and beliefs. In Chosŏn, in part due to *sirhak,* doctrinaire neo-Confucianism had begun to lose some of its authority. Also, Chosŏn's rigid social scheme seemed to be creaking at the seams. As knowledge and mobility increased, the ills of class oppression, social exploitation, poverty, and illness, and not least Chosŏn's ongoing curse of slavery, became more visible. As in China, the population increase strained existing resources and created a sense of impoverishment compared with earlier times. The relationship between China and Korea, which for so long had been shaped within a set of distinct ideas about international order, were coming under pressure from within and without.

2

The Internationalization of East Asia

China, Korea, and the World, 1866–1992

In the first part of the nineteenth century the world began to change very fast. Steamships and railways transformed distance, so that what was once far suddenly seemed near. New products and new weapons emerged from factories, setting up markets and conquests. Inside China new ideas started to take root, upsetting old certainties and creating divisions and unrest. The defeat by Britain in 1843 opened up for new questions being asked, especially among those who had witnessed the defeat. Between 1850 and 1868 a wave of rebellions swept the Qing empire, all inspired by religious visions. The Taiping armies—coming from a movement that called itself Christian and was inspired by a dramatic new reading of the Bible—challenged the Qing for power. At least 20 million people died in southern China as the Taiping armies first advanced and then were slowly suppressed by forces loyal to the empire.

But little changed in the relationship between Qing and Chosŏn, at least not for a long time. Emissaries, missions, and representations continued to travel from Seoul to Beijing, inquiring after the emperor's health and the advances of his empire. Although there was restlessness in Korean society and even members of the elite were beginning to ask new questions about how the world worked, the elite majority and the king stuck with the old ways, believing that any change would be for the worse. They were conservative because of what they believed in, but also for practical reasons: They feared giving in to outside pressure, letting in new religions and new ideas about how to organize society. They were afraid that rebellions among the population could threaten the correctness of the state. And they feared changes in Chosŏn's relations with the Qing empire, believing that the Qing could return to its aggressive ways of the past. From the perspective of Korea's leaders, it seemed as if change could bring no good.

When the Chosŏn elite looked at China in the midnineteenth century, their worst suspicions were confirmed. The Christian and Muslim rebellions there proved the nefariousness of Western religions and convinced many Koreans that missionaries and converts were the advance troops of foreign-made confusion. From the early nineteenth century on, the Chosŏn state engaged in intense anti-Christian campaigns, which grew in strength as the number of Korean believers increased. Some of the Christians executed were Chinese who had gone to Chosŏn as missionaries. In 1839 three French missionaries were publicly beheaded in Seoul. Although many Koreans were attracted by new religions, or maybe because of that, the state became increasingly repressive as the Western presence in China increased.

Like in China, Korea also saw a number of syncretic new religions appear as a result of foreign inspiration. The most important of these, by far, was the Tonghak movement, which originated around 1860, in the wake of the Taiping rebellion and the second Opium War. Its founder, Ch'oe Che-u, had been impressed by those who claimed that "Western learning" would be the future of Korea, but he felt that Koreans needed their own version of the new forms of thinking. "A strange rumor spread throughout the land," Ch'oe wrote, "that Westerners had discovered the truth and there was nothing they could not do. Nothing could stand before their military power. Even China was being destroyed. Will our country, too, suffer the same fate? . . . Is it possible that they know the Heavenly Order and have received the Heavenly Mandate?"[1] Ch'oe's response was Tonghak ("Eastern Learning"), which he claimed was given him in direct revelations by the Lord of Heaven. Ch'oe was arrested and executed in 1863, but his Tonghak, which blended neo-Confucian ideas with Christianity and Buddhism, with a strong emphasis on egalitarianism, survived him and spread among peasants in southeastern Korea, from where it would make a comeback thirty years later.

The revolutions and wars in China during the 1850s and early 1860s made a very strong impression on Chosŏn leaders. The first clashes with the West that the Qing lost could be seen as a passing phase—after all, the Qing had been challenged before and come back strong—but the second wave of losses was much harder to write off. "The West wins if it fights, and if it

attacks, there is nothing that it cannot achieve," commented one Korean observer.[2] After the Western sack of the old Summer Palace in Beijing in 1860 and the emperor's flight to Manchuria, the Chosŏn government met for emergency sessions. They first decided to send a delegation to inquire after the emperor's well-being. Then they began planning to strengthen border defenses

MAP 2.1 Qing Empire, c. 1750

and defenses of the main ports. First and foremost they had to find out more about what was happening. "Despite the rather different size, [Chosŏn] to the Qing Dynasty is what the teeth are to the lips," said one report. "If Qing is in trouble, our country would suffer. . . . What we should do now is to visit the assaulted venues . . . to ascertain the real situation. This is comparable to what we should do to prevent contracting illness—asking a patient with the same disease about its causes."[3]

But despite the obvious danger, neo-Confucian traditionalists confirmed their worldview. Yi Hang-no, who was both a defender of orthodoxy and a sharp critic of Chosŏn's social ills, memorably summed up the traditionalist position toward China and the Sino-Korean relationship, reconfirming the fundamental Confucian tenets as set out in the basic texts:

When Chinese civilization encounters a barbarian people, the barbarians are transformed by Chinese ways into a civilized people. Barbarians look up to China and are delighted to receive its civilizing influence. This is the way things are, this is the natural order of things. This is the way human beings ought to feel. China is like the root, a plant supplying nourishment for the branches and leaves. It is like the hands and feet that protect the belly and chest of the human body. This can never change. . . .

These Europeans come from a land far away from China, so it is only natural that their customs are quite different from Chinese customs. Like children of peasant households, though they study Confucian writings as hard as they can, they can never grasp the structure and organization of those writings as well as children from families that have been studying Confucianism for generations.

Unfortunately the world is such a big place that Europe had no contact with China for quite a long time. This means, regrettably, that Europe was not introduced to the basic principles of the Great Dao, and Europeans were not turned into more virtuous people by its civilizing power. Europeans do have a remarkable talent for technology. They easily surpass the Chinese in that area. But that achievement makes them arrogant, and they think that they can convert the whole world to their way of thinking. They need to think again!

The heavens are so vast that the universe appears boundless. Yet we can locate the center of the universe, that point around which it revolves. That is the North Star. The earth is also quite large, extending so far in all directions that it too appears infinite in size. Yet it also has a center, the site from which the entire earth is governed. That terrestrial center is China. There are also many different ways human beings can behave and interact, so many that they appear countless. But above them all is the Supreme Ultimate, the Way of Ways. The North Pole rules over the multitude of stars, so the multitude of stars all bow in the direction of the North Pole. The earth rules the ten thousand regions, so all of those regions recognize the paramount position of China. This is the one principle that unites everything in Heaven, on earth, and among people.[4]

But Yi's declarations of principle could not change the real situation. China, or at least the Qing empire, was in decline as an international power. As imperialist pressure on the Qing and on Tokugawa Japan increased, Chosŏn was also coming under threat. The government followed the same routine every time

European vessels showed up at its doorstep: It turned them away and reported the incident to the Qing in order for Beijing to protest on its behalf. But in 1866 this policy of avoidance no longer worked. After four French missionaries were caught and executed, France threatened to invade. Yi Ha-ŭng, known as the Taewŏngun (Prince of the High Court), who ruled Chosŏn on behalf of his son, King Kojong, decided to resist. The regime hunkered down. Those who urged compromise were purged or executed. Leaders like Yi Hang-no joined the regime in resistance. The French landed with about 800 troops at Kanghwa Island, downriver from Seoul, but were contained by Korean troops and forced to withdraw without having accomplished much, except the looting of Chosŏn storehouses on the island. But, in all its theatricality, it was a sign of more to come. When the French insisted to Beijing that Chosŏn negotiate a treaty with them, the Qing bureaucracy simply passed the request on to Seoul without comment. The Taewŏngun and his supporters were shocked: China seemed no longer willing, or able, to stand up for its vassal.[5]

The attempt by the US vessel *General Sherman* to sail into Pyongyang in northern Korea the same year confirmed the Taewŏngun's views. He ordered the ship to leave, and, when the captain refused and fired into the crowd, he directed that it be destroyed. Another US attempt five years later, this time with five warships, also failed to achieve its purpose of forcing Korea to open trade relations, though almost 250 Koreans were killed in fighting after the Americans tried to land near Seoul.[6] But the biggest danger for the Taewŏngun's policy came from Japan. After a coup in 1868, the so-called Meiji Restoration, Japan's new leaders copied Western attempts to force Korea to open up. And the Japanese were close enough and, gradually, powerful enough, to force a change in Chosŏn's approach to international affairs. With no aid from the Qing forthcoming and with the Japanese landing at several places along the coast, the young King Kojong in 1876 decided to negotiate directly with the Japanese. The outcome was the Treaty of Kanghwa, which opened several Korean ports to Japanese trade and guaranteed Japan the right to extraterritoriality in Korea. In spite of Chosŏn being called an autonomous state in the treaty, the Qing did not protest. They had enough with their own trouble.

The Coming of Japan

As Japan established a presence in Chosŏn, many young Koreans, including the king, were impressed and horrified in equal amounts by the technological aspects of its power. The advice they were getting from China was to quickly establish relations with Western powers as well, both to check Japanese influence but also follow the Qing pattern of self-strengthening: to learn from the West in order to better check the West's ambitions. Against much resistance at home, Kojong began following the Chinese advice. He sent missions to both China and Japan to learn more about new knowledge and technologies that had arrived from the West. During the 1880s the king followed a dual policy of negotiating with foreign powers, but to do so assisted by the Qing and, if possible, in China, so that the empire would still have a sense of responsibility for Chosŏn's foreign relations. By 1888 Chosŏn had signed treaties giving trading rights to all major foreign powers, including the Qing empire itself.[7]

The policy of gradual opening led to strong resistance in Korea. More than 10,000 Confucian scholars signed a letter of protest directly to the king, in which they claimed that letting the foreigners in would destroy Korean propriety and righteousness. In 1882, part of the military around Seoul rebelled, killed a number of Japanese and Korean reformers, and tried to force the king to abrogate all foreign treaties. The rebellion was quelled by Qing troops, and Beijing left a contingent of soldiers in Seoul to support King Kojong. Two years later a group of radical Korean reformers attempted to seize power, supported by Japanese forces. The coup failed when Qing troops intervened, but the fighting between Qing and Japanese forces in Seoul frightened both governments enough to have them make a deal on reciprocal withdrawal of their armies from Korea. The Chinese general Yuan Shikai was left in place, though, as the chief adviser to the Korean king.[8]

Yuan Shikai's policy, during all of his almost ten years in Seoul, was to move toward a new form of Chosŏn dependency on the Qing empire. He realized that the old suzerainty was gone, but imagined it replaced by a relationship that was not entirely different from that between European countries and their colonies. The Qing, Yuan argued, had to learn from the Westerners how to become a modern empire with foreign possessions and commercial interests.[9] His main fear was that Japanese or Russian control of Korea would lead to an imperialist encirclement of China. King Kojong soon had more than enough of what he regarded as Yuan's overbearing insolence. He approached the Russians (and probably also the Japanese) to rescue him from Yuan's tight embrace. The king had tasted reform and autonomy, and liked both. Now he felt that the Qing was preventing Korea's further progress. Yuan Shikai, in his reports to Beijing, realized that he was sitting on a powder keg, but hoped the force of his personality and the threat of Qing intervention could prevent it from exploding.

What lit the fuse was an event hard to foresee. In early 1894 members of the Tonghak movement organized a rebellion in southwestern Korea, demanding tax relief, land reform, execution of corrupt officials, and the expulsion of all Westerners and Japanese. They were soon joined by other groups that were dissatisfied with the status quo, becoming an immediate threat to the survival of the Chosŏn state. In spite of his conflicts with Yuan Shikai, King Kojong saw no other way out than calling for the Qing to intervene. After the arrival of Qing troops, the rebellion receded. But Japan used the opportunity to send its own invasion force. This time the aim was to wrestle control of Korea from the Qing and set it on the path to reform under Japanese leadership. The Japanese forces quickly seized control of Seoul. Kojong declared a plan for thorough reform and modernization of Chosŏn, helped by Japanese advisers. He also, probably more reluctantly, called on the Japanese to ally with Chosŏn against the Qing.

The war that followed was a disaster for the Qing empire. Not only did it lose control of Korea. It also had to cede Taiwan to the Japanese, give them extended trade and settlement privileges in Manchuria, and pay huge war reparations. And yet some Qing officials believed they had gotten off lightly. If it had not been for counterpressure by envious Western powers, Japan would have received even greater privileges. By the time the war ended in 1895, Japanese forces not only controlled the Manchurian coast but also had taken control of parts of Shandong and advanced to within 300 miles of Beijing. Most of the dead in the war were Chinese and Korean, with Chinese military losses around 40,000. The Japanese only lost 1,100 men. Most importantly, the Qing loss in the Sino-Japanese War was demonstrable and for everyone to see. The China-centered order in eastern Asia was dead, even though most Koreans found the new disorder very difficult to come to terms with.

The effects of the war on elites in both China and Korea were profound. Most informed people, including in Europe and the United States, had expected the Qing to win; it had size, proximity, and a large program of military self-strengthening on its side. Koreans who were forced to work for or with the Japanese military expected China to rescue them. Even the Korean reformers, who sympathized with Japan and often joined its cause, thought the outcome was at best uncertain. The decisive military victory for Japan meant that the Chosŏn leaders had to reconfigure their thinking about where Korea fit in an eastern Asian context. Understanding the new constellation and figuring out how power was divided among the many states that now operated in their neighborhood was a life-or-death issue for them.

By the late 1890s the concept of nationhood in a form that connected directly to Western discourse started to find its way into Korea. Just like the Tonghak in its way had attempted to define what it meant to be Korean (as opposed to Japanese or inside the empire), intellectuals tried to make use of what they learned abroad. Yu Kil-chun, in his 1895 book *Things Seen and Heard in Travels to the West,* defined the European terms "nation" and "patriotism" and found them remarkably similar to Korean ideals. For Yu, who had studied in Japan and the United States and had traveled in Europe, Korean nationalism could easily incorporate or even embody specific neo-Confucian ideals.[10] But in order for the links between Confucian practices and modern Korean nationhood to be fully established, Korea's new nationalists had to create a break with *sadae,* Korean neo-Confucianism's traditional subservience to the ideal (if not always the reality) of China. The Independence Club, one of the new nationalist organizations, argued that Koreans needed to break the "aristocratic cultural slavery to Chinese culture."[11] Some wanted to break the bonds with Chinese Confucianism altogether and forget "the boasted classics which have striven for three thousand years to elevate Korea [but] have only plunged her deeper and deeper into the mire."[12]

Instead of *sadae,* and instead of new forms of subservience to Japan or to the West, the new Korean nationalists argued for a revitalization of indigenous culture through the use of the Korean alphabet to educate the people. "If we exerted ourselves [Korea] could become an enlightened, strong, and prosperous nation. . . . If from today, the people, joining hands together, work to preserve its independence forever, then their descendants can perform their functions as the people of a worthy nation."[13] "We must become servants to truth and righteousness. We must become an army in the service of our own true spirit. . . . If we look only at the outer manifestation of our situation today, it is not something we want passed on to our children. But a different current runs beneath; it is the true spirit of the people and lies in all aspects of the nation."[14] For the new generation of Korean nationalists, the nation was synonymous with Korea's unique spiritual strength and the righteousness that fueled it.

For the Korean nation to manifest itself, nationalists of different kinds argued for a strong and capable state, which could modernize the country and rectify its ills. Some writers attacked the Confucian social order, accusing it of being authoritarian, patriarchal, and uniquely oppressive toward women and young people. But others believed that some form of Korean Confucianism could be rescued as a guideline for the new state under the leadership of the king. These two opposing trends in Korean nationalism were there from the beginning in the 1890s, although the allegiance of individuals in the first generation often shifted between them, as did elite political and foreign affiliations. Very much like in China, it was a confusing age, in which all that had seemed certain and durable evaporated in quick succession. No wonder that one factional affiliation or even one identity did not seem enough for inquisitive Korean students of a new world.

The political situation itself did not promote personal or ideological stability. In 1894 Korean reformers and their Japanese advisers worked together to deliver an ambitious program of change. The so-called Kabo reforms, which King Kojong ratified, meant, finally, the abolition of slavery and a new style of government with departments and a cabinet-style leadership, which the king had to consult. The country was divided into new administrative units that broke the political control of the Korean gentry. Taxes were made more equitable and the tax system centralized, and a new monetary system linked to the Japanese currency was introduced. The Kabo reforms met with much resistance in Korea, in part because of their innovations and in part because they were connected with Japan. The queen felt that the royal house was giving up too much power, and criticized Japan openly. The king, as often before, vacillated between embracing the new and being skeptical of foreign influence. As the reforms began to stall, and emboldened by their country's military victories, a group of Japanese diplomats and officers decided to assassinate Queen Min because of her opposition to the reforms. The Japanese broke into the royal palace in October 1895 and murdered the queen in front of her horrified companions at court.

The murder of Queen Min was the first case of blatant Japanese overreach that was going to blight the country's involvement with the rest of Asia for over a generation. It led to Korean resistance and political chaos. King Kojong fled to the Russian embassy, where he remained for more than a year, marking Russia's real entry into Korean politics. Over the next decade Japanese leaders tried to solidify their influence in Korea, but met resistance from Russia, other imperialist powers, the Qing, and not least the Koreans themselves. King Kojong managed to get himself declared emperor of a new Empire of Korea, stressing equality in status with his Qing and Japanese counterparts. But the new independent empire's room for maneuver decreased by the year. The Qing state was focused on its own internal battles and on handling Western and Japanese imperialism inside China itself. And Japan's increasing power in the region made it increasingly more difficult for Korean leaders to resist Japanese demands. A British visitor noted, "Japan has abolished the impalpable suzerainty of China only to replace it by a palpable and selfish domination of her own."[15]

Even though the Qing had been forced to accept Korean independence in principle, and irrespective of the relative lack of attention to Korean affairs in Beijing, imperial officials continued to worry about what the future might bring. If Japan were to annex Korea, one official argued, "all the [vassals] of our dynasty would be subordinate to foreign barbarians, so other countries would encroach on China's inner land, and consequently Xinjiang, Taiwan, Tibet, and Manchuria would be in grave danger."[16] Another stressed that Korea was China's fence. "If the fence collapsed, Mukden [Shenyang] would be in great danger. Chosŏn, which is different from Vietnam and Burma, which are thousands of miles away from China, is mutually dependent with China, like the lips and the teeth, and like bones and flesh."[17] But Qing attempts at appealing to tradition and common heritage in dealing with the new Korean state paid few dividends.

Kojong's attempts to rescue Korean independence by involving other great powers were also unsuccessful. In 1904–1905 Japan fought another war over the future on Korea and all of Northeast Asia, this time against Russia. Yet again the Japanese were widely expected to lose, and still they won the war, marking the first time since the late seventeenth century that an Asian power had decisively won a military conflict against Europeans. The outcome of the Russo-Japanese War in many ways sealed Korea's fate. Not only did it leave Japan by far the most powerful state in the region. It also strengthened Japanese elites' belief that in order to keep their prime position, they would have to bring Korea under total control. Similar to ten years before, the Western powers forced Japan to give up many of its gains from the war. Amid large-scale protests in Japan against a peace settlement that provided neither extensive territory nor reparations, Japanese leaders forced Kojong to make Korea a protectorate of Japan, with all responsibility for military and foreign affairs to rest with Tokyo. In 1907, after he had appealed to other powers for help in protecting Korean independence, Kojong was pressured by the Japanese to abdicate in favor of his son. In 1910 Japan unilaterally annexed the country outright. "His Majesty the Emperor of Korea," said the annexation treaty, "makes the complete and permanent cession to His Majesty the Emperor of Japan of all rights of sovereignty over the whole of Korea." After 500 years the Chosŏn state was no more.

For the Qing the full Japanese annexation of Korea was what they had dreaded most. And yet they were incapable of countering it. By 1910, domestic strife in China was again on the rise, and the government tried to crack down on criticism, including of their inaction in Korea. For many Chinese, the inability of the Qing to resist Japan's takeover of Korea was a sure sign that they had lost the mandate to rule. In spite of press censorship, the government was attacked both directly and indirectly. The newspaper *Minxu Ribao* (which was subsequently closed down by the Qing censors) had already in 1909 commented that "given its geographical location, it has always been clear that Chosŏn would be at the center of the struggle between countries to become the hegemonic power in East Asia. . . . When we factor in the need for the establishment of equal interests amongst the foreign powers, it becomes evident that our vast empire will eventually be divided into dozens of Chosŏns. Today we mourn Chosŏn's fate. However, there is real concern that others may be mourning for us in the very near future."[18] After the annexation, another Chinese newspaper reprinted a letter from a young Korean to a high-ranking Qing official:

> Korea, a land which for thousands of years was a vassal of China, has now fallen into ruin. Having nowhere to express my grief, I present this mournful letter to you, a member of the imperial family of Qing, to make public my ardent desire for the further development of Qing's civilization and its eventual liberation and subsequent protection of the territory of its former vassal. . . . The collapse of Korea should be of deep concern for Qing, a country that we regard as being the equivalent of our fatherland. . . . The close geographic proximity between Korea and China raises the concern that the annexation of Korea could result in a case of "the teeth getting cold now that the lips are gone." . . . Well aware that little can be done for Korea, which already lies in ruins, I nevertheless find myself hoping against all hope that your country (Qing) will help us repel the Japanese invasion and regain our nation by strengthening its military capacity and harnessing the power of its 400 million citizens.[19]

But critics also insisted that China had to draw direct political and diplomatic lessons of the Chosŏn collapse. The newspaper *Shenbao* argued, "Our government appears to have been caught off guard. . . . [It] should seek to quell other countries' ambitions by greatly improving our political system and rallying public sentiment."[20] Its rival, *Shibao*, found that "Japan forced China to abandon its historical role as protector of Korea on the grounds that it was seeking to preserve the latter's independence. However, rather than protecting Korea's independence, Japan instead proceeded to swallow it whole. As such, its calls for the independence of Korea were in fact little more than a ruse designed to foster its own designs on its unfortunate neighbor. This method used by France in conjunction with Vietnam in the past has now been employed by Japan with regards to Korea."[21]

When the Qing empire finally collapsed in 1912, part of the criticism shared by all of its Chinese opponents was that it had squandered China's international status. From the very beginning, Chinese nationalism in the making—as its proponents were defending China's interests against foreign imperialists— had a dual relationship to Korea (or, for that matter, Vietnam, Mongolia, or Tibet). On the one hand, Chinese nationalists, such as the first president of the Republic of China, Sun Yat-sen, genuinely sympathized with nationalists in Korea and wanted to furnish them with practical support. On the other hand, they regarded all these countries as having a special relationship with China because of their former status as vassals of the empire. For the first generation of Chinese nationalists, defining China posed profound challenges with regard to history, culture, and political purpose.

Nationalism in Exile

For Koreans, the fifteen years after the Sino-Japanese War had been a whirlwind of shocks and disappointments. The end result was an unprecedented calamity for which Koreans blamed not only the Japanese, but also China and themselves. The Japanese were seen as rapacious and brutal, but also as dynamic, bold, and well ordered. China under the Qing was seen as backward and lethargic. And Korean elites increasingly saw their own past as a kind of unworldly fantasy, not suited for present-day conditions. By adhering to it, they had failed the nation. After 1910, some chose to collaborate with Japan out of self-interest or because they hoped to build a stronger Korea in the future. Others went into exile or attempted to build a national consciousness in Korea, in theory more often than in practice. For almost all, the key tragedy was that their country had been annexed just as modern Korean nationalism was coming into full force. Although Koreans drew different lessons from their past, this incongruity would ensure that their concept of nation was surrounded by an intensity of vision rarely found elsewhere.[22]

The very fact that the resistance to Japanese occupation had to be mainly formed outside of Korea provided added passion to the cause. Korean exiles gathered in Shanghai, Vladivostok, and Manchuria. Some went to the United States, including the young Syngman Rhee (Yi Sŭng-man), the first Korean to receive a PhD from an American university. The shock of annexation was deep, and it took time before the resistance groups in exile began to coalesce into full-fledged movements. In China, some of the Koreans in exile worked closely with radical Chinese nationalists who were disappointed with the first republican governments' willingness to give in to Japanese pressure. Yuan Shikai, the former Qing representative to Korea who now reappeared as president of the Chinese republic, was a particular object of loathing for Koreans and Chinese radicals alike, especially after 1915, when he accepted Japan's demands to have more influence in China.

In Korea itself, the aim of the Japanese administrators and the Koreans who collaborated with them was to create a modern, efficient, and productive region as part of the new empire. The first task was to stamp out the widespread open opposition to the new order. This the Japanese army and police did ruthlessly and methodically. In the mountains, resistance groups that often called themselves "The Righteous Army" were hunted down by a combination of Japanese military efficiency and the recruitment of well-paid and well-informed Korean scouts. In the towns strict censorship and curfews were imposed, and residents were subjected to a barrage of Japanese-inspired propaganda about the wealth and power of the new ruling country. The message to all Koreans was clear: Only by working with Japan could the ideals of Korean modernity be realized, and only in a community with Japan could Koreans feel safe.

The physical transformation of Korea during the four decades of Japanese control was indeed stunning. Communications were revolutionized through roads and railroads, radio and telegraph. Food production was improved, though much of the food was exported to other parts of the Japanese empire. Industrial production, which had slowly begun in the 1890s, became widespread, especially in the north. Basic education was made mandatory, and a university and technical colleges were constructed. New and comprehensive laws and regulations were applied by a newly trained colonial judiciary. The Japanese and their supporters claimed that the new Korea was everything that China and old Korea was not. For them, Koreans had stepped from a zone of darkness into the light of modernity.

But in spite of their efficiency as rulers, Japanese leaders struggled with determining what exact status Koreans were to have in the new empire. Korea was an integral part of Japan—not a colony, but a region under special administration. Koreans were subjects of the Japanese emperor, but not fully Japanese citizens. They should aspire to become Japanese, but it was left unclear how that process would work. Like modern European empires, Japan wanted to control, modernize, and improve imperial subjects according to their own standards, but feared the consequences of full integration. As a result, Koreans were always treated as second class in their own country, never mind in Japan or elsewhere in the empire. Throughout the colonial era, privileges in Korea were given to Japanese, who soon owned half of all land in the country and completely dominated the professions and industries.

Under these circumstances it was no surprise that resistance resurfaced among Koreans. In 1919 widespread nationalist protest broke out. Kojong died that year, and many Koreans preferred to mourn him in public as a great national leader rather than as the vacillating and uncertain king and emperor he had been. On March 1, Korean nationalists read out a declaration of independence in Seoul:

We hereby declare that Korea is an independent state and that Koreans are a self-governing people. We proclaim it to the nations of the world in affirmation of the principle of the equality of all nations, and we proclaim it to our posterity, preserving in perpetuity the right of national survival. We make this declaration on the strength of five thousand years of history as an expression of the devotion and loyalty of twenty million people.[23]

But when Korean leaders in exile tried to get international acceptance for their views at the peace conferences after World War One, they were given short shrift. Japan had participated on the winning side in the war, and no Western country wanted to antagonize Japan over Korea, especially because any such action might have called attention to the demands of subjects in their own colonial empires. Appeals for Chinese intercession also fell on deaf ears, even if the Korean independence declaration had noted that the Chinese "constitute the main axis for stability in the East."[24] For many Koreans, as for many Chinese, the aftermath of the Great War was a time of great disappointment for their national ambitions. It seemed as if the road to sovereign, independent, and unified statehood was closed to them, just when US president Woodrow Wilson declared political self-determination to be a universal right for all nations. When the president in 1918 had proclaimed, on America's behalf, that "our passion for justice and for self-government is . . . a passion which, once set in action, must be satisfied," many Asians had hoped that America's fervor for freedom also encompassed them.[25] By the early 1920s such hopes of assistance from the West had been put in abeyance, at least by Koreans who suffered under Japan's increasingly strong hold on their country.

As Koreans moved beyond disappointments with Wilsonian practices, two new directions in their national aspirations started to appear. The first was an increased emphasis on armed resistance. After the Japanese crackdown on the March 1 movement, in which at least 7,000 Koreans were killed, guerrilla groups started operating against Japan, both in Korea itself and abroad. Most of these groups were centered in Manchuria, where many Koreans had been moving since the nineteenth century and to which some independence groups now retreated. In 1920 these Korean armed groups had their first engagements with Japanese troops who had entered Manchuria and eastern Russia during the Russian civil war. Although Korean sources often grossly exaggerate the number of Japanese killed in such actions, the very fact that Koreans were now fighting in Manchuria was of great importance to the independence movement, and buoyed the nascent exile government of a Republic of Korea, which had been set up in Shanghai in 1919.

The second new direction was the effect the Russian October Revolution of 1917 had on independence-minded Koreans. Just like among Chinese or Southeast Asians, the Bolshevik message of freedom from imperialism and the development of backward countries through collective, state-centered action fit the thinking of many Koreans. The new Union of Soviet Socialist Republics (USSR, or Soviet Union) gave hope for a different kind of future for Korea and for China, as well. Although some exiled Koreans viewed the Bolsheviks as too radical or too Western in their approach, others saw a form of organization, and a view of the world, that could be fit to Korean values. The first Korean Communists struggled with Marxist materialism—their neo-Confucian background did not lend itself well to the belief that the world was based on material progress and class struggles. But as long as Soviet or Chinese Marxists presented them with the tools, theoretical and practical, for fighting the Japanese occupation, they were happy to learn.

Like the other nationalist movements, Korean Communism grew up in exile. The first Communists were part of Chinese or Soviet groups in Manchuria, Siberia, or the Russian Pacific. Aleksandra Kim (Kim Aerim), born in Siberia, became head of foreign affairs for the Far East bureau of the Russian Bolshevik Party, and a co-founder of the Korean Socialist Party, which was set up in Khabarovsk in April 1918. Later that year Kim was captured by Russian counterrevolutionaries and their Japanese advisers and executed.[26] By 1921 there were two Korean Communist parties, one based in Irkutsk and another one in Shanghai. The Moscow-based Communist International (Comintern) tried to organize a single Korean Communist organization, but found factionalism among Korean Communists difficult to overcome. The Chinese Communist Party, founded in 1921 by young Chinese who had been attracted to the Russian Revolution in ways similar to their Korean comrades, started accepting Korean members from the very beginning, and Koreans served as liaisons between the Chinese party and Moscow. Chinese Communists, along with other radical

Chinese nationalists, set up a Sino-Korean Mutual Assistance Association; the young Mao Zedong was one of the leaders of its branch in his home province of Hunan.[27]

But being a Korean Communist, either inside Korea or in exile, was no simple matter. The persecution of Communists in Korea intensified in the late 1920s and 1930s, and many of those who avoided prison had to flee abroad. Meanwhile, Japanese power was extending further and further into Manchuria, making the Communist existence there precarious. Factional infighting among the Korean Communists themselves complicated matters, to the point that the Comintern decided to close down all Korean Communist organizations in China and make Korean Communists join the Chinese Communist Party (CCP).[28] One of those who joined, in 1931, was the young Kim Il-sung, a Communist born in Korea but raised in Manchuria. Then, in the mid-1930s, both the CCP and the Soviet Communists turned on the Koreans, suspecting many among them of being spies for Japan. In the CCP most Koreans were purged from their positions. In the USSR they fared much worse: In Stalin's purges, in relative terms more Korean Communists were executed than members of any other population group. In 1937 all Koreans in the Soviet Far East were deported to Central Asia out of an absurd fear that they might cooperate with the Japanese in case of an invasion.

While their infighting ensured that Korean Communists would remain a minority among nationalists, at least for the time being, the government of the Republic of Korea in exile had its own troubles. Syngman Rhee, who had been named president when he was still in the United States, came to Shanghai to head the government, but left after a few months to return to America, where he thought he could do more for the nationalist cause. After he was impeached and removed as president in 1925, the government in exile went through a turbulent period, with a number of leaders and much conflict.

But while the Korean nationalists in exile were squabbling among themselves, China started moving toward more unity. Sun Yat-sen, the head of the Guomindang (GMD)—the Chinese National People's Party—had an unlikely return as leader of a popular anti-imperialist political movement, supported by the Soviets and in alliance with the small Chinese Communist Party. Sun hoped to restore China's centrality in the eastern Asian region, if possible also in an alliance with Japan. In a speech in Japan in 1924, the year before he died, Sun Yat-sen challenged his audience to become leaders for the emancipation of Asia. Studiously avoiding mentioning Korea, the pragmatic Sun attacked the West's "rule of might," as he called it, and heaped praise on Japan's modernization. China, he said, was weak and divided, but it respected benevolence and virtue, the "rule of right." "The rule of right always influences people with justice and reason, while the rule of might always oppresses people with brute force and military measures. People who are influenced by justice and virtue will never forget their superior State, even if that country has become weak. So Nepal even now willingly respects China as a superior State." The choice before the Japanese, Sun said, was "whether Japan will be the hawk of the Western civilization of the rule of might, or the tower of strength of the Orient."[29]

Korean nationalists, and quite a few Chinese, were horrified at Sun's outreach to Japan. But Sun's ability to put together coalitions ensured the continued popularity of his movement. There was simply no other organization around into which young Chinese could put their nationalist urges. Sun promised his followers a nation instead of an empire, but a nation with special qualities and a special position in Asia. First the Western imperialist positions in China and those ("warlords," Sun called them) who believed in regional autonomy had to be crushed. With Soviet assistance, Sun prepared for a "northern expedition" from his Guangzhou headquarters in order to reunify China. Koreans living in China saw the GMD's northward march as part of the future liberation of their homeland. More than 800 Koreans signed up to participate and many more hoped to join as the expedition entered the north.

But Sun was better at talking than fighting. He decided to go to Beijing for a final attempt at negotiations with his northern rivals. While there he was taken ill and died, at fifty-eight, with the succession in the GMD very unclear. The man who emerged as the military leader of the movement, Chiang Kai-shek, pushed for the northern expedition to begin even without its key guide. As the Chinese nationalists, with the Communist contingent within them, moved north, they used the martyrdom of their prophet and the excesses of Western imperialism as their banners. By 1927 the GMD had taken most of southern China, including Shanghai. Chiang and his supporters turned on the Communists and drove the party underground, while insisting that all groups, including Koreans and other foreign fighters, submit to the absolute authority of the GMD under Chiang's leadership.

As the Guomindang established their control of China, Koreans found their room for maneuver limited. Chiang Kai-shek was sympathetic toward the Korean liberation struggle, but he wanted to control the exile government and make Korean leaders subsume their aims under those he laid out for China. Chiang wanted to avoid Korean provocations in China that could lead to a confrontation with Japan. Ito Hirobumi, one of the founding fathers of modern Japan and resident general in Korea, was assassinated by a Korean in Manchuria in 1909. In 1932, after Japanese and Chinese forces had clashed in Shanghai, a young Korean there set off a bomb that killed the commander of the Japanese troops as well as a visiting Japanese minister. Chiang praised the attack in private, but avoided any public comment on it.[30] In all there were over 300 Korean attacks on Japanese targets in China in the 1920s and 1930s, in addition to Korean military units fighting in Manchuria.

By 1932 it was clear that China and Japan were heading toward conflict. The Japanese saw China's unification under the GMD as an immediate threat to their privileged position in eastern Asia, and moved to take full control of Manchuria, where they had gradually extended their power in the 1920s. To some in the Korean resistance, Tokyo's selection of the last Qing emperor as the new leader of its Manchurian satellite, which it called Manchukuo, was entirely predictable. Now, claimed the Korean Provisional Government, as it mobilized to set up its own military force, the Korean Liberation Army, the true Chinese and the Koreans were allies again, as they had always been in past. Chiang Kai-shek did not think much of the military power of his Korean allies but was glad for all help that he could get. To the disappointment of the Koreans, however, the Chinese leader never extended formal recognition to their government in exile.

The gradual Japanese takeover of Manchuria made life very dangerous for the Korean Communist units who operated there. While the Chinese Communists went to join their comrades south of the Great Wall, many of the Koreans went north to join with the Soviets. Among the last ones to operate in Manchuria was Kim Il-sung and his small group of guerrillas. They crossed over into the USSR in 1940, where Kim retrained as a Soviet army captain in the 88th rifle brigade, but his group otherwise sat idle until 1945. Koreans abroad who wanted to fight the Japanese ended up having (at least) three choices: enlisting with the Korean provisional government, with the Chinese Communists, or with the Soviets. During the 1930s, Korean exile politics became increasingly factional, with foreign sponsors lining up to support "their" Koreans.

The majority of Koreans, of course, had very little choice in the matter. After a less brutal period in Japanese colonial control in the 1920s, government oppression increased again in the 1930s, as Japan's conflicts with other powers intensified. While the exile movements celebrated Japan's increasing isolation after the takeover of Manchuria, Koreans at home struggled with the hundreds of day-to-day compromises they had to make with the occupiers in order to live a reasonably normal life. Some chose the path of resistance, but an increasing number bought into the ideology of imperial Japan—a common future in which education, technology, military prowess, and a strong state were guarantees against Western decadence and Chinese dissolution. Opting wholly for Japan was, in a way, easier than the intermediate position that so many Koreans had held up to the mid-1930s. One young Korean who embraced the Japanese message was Park Chung-hee, who trained as an officer in Manchukuo and in Japan, and then joined the fight against Communists in Manchuria.

Koreans faced many difficult choices at home and in Japan, and their position was even more ambivalent in Manchuria and Taiwan. By 1945 over two million Koreans had moved into Manchukuo, where they farmed or engaged in business, often supported by their status as Japanese subjects. Some Koreans were proud of their success in Manchuria because they regarded it as ancient Korean land. Understandably, the increased Korean presence under Japanese protection led to clashes with the Chinese, with several violent incidents in Manchuria. In Korea, Chinese were attacked in perceived revenge for Chinese attacks on Koreans north of the border. Only a very small number of Koreans were in Taiwan, but there, too, they were in an ambiguous position: one the one hand seen as Japanese agents by the Chinese, and on the other exploited by Japan, as were Korean women who were forced into sex slavery at Japanese military bases on Taiwan.

The War against Japan

After full-scale war between Japan and China broke out in 1937, and especially after the beginning of the Pacific War in 1941, Korea began suffering the consequences of Japan's imperial overstretch. Oppression inside Korea was worse than ever, with Japanese authorities attempting a cultural genocide against Koreans, forcing everyone to take Japanese names and prohibiting the teaching of Korean in schools. Koreans were forced into labor units for the Japanese army and an increasing number were recruited as soldiers. About five million Koreans served in work brigades, 250,000 served as soldiers, and at least 100,000 were forced into sex slavery. More than 25,000 Koreans died fighting for Japan.[31]

While Koreans at home suffered, the spread of Japanese aggression meant new opportunities for Korean nationalists in exile. Now they could argue that Korea was but Japan's first victim, and that the real Japanese aims were to take over Asia and the Pacific. Syngman Rhee, now back in the United States, claimed that like in the late sixteenth century, Korea was simply a springboard for Japan's plans to conquer China. He tried to get the Americans to offer recognition and support to the Koreans—himself first and foremost—but without much success, to begin with. The government in exile had more luck with Chiang Kai-shek and the Guomindang. Chiang became increasingly aware that support for Korea was not only a duty but a practical necessity for China. He aimed at rebuilding China's position in Asia after the war was over. And a Korea tightly aligned with the Republic of China was an essential part of any such plan. In 1934, as the war with Japan was brewing, Chiang had written in his diary: "Recover Taiwan and Korea. Recover the land that was originally part of the Han and Tang dynasty. Then, as descendants of the Yellow Emperor, we will have no shame."[32]

Uneasy as they sometimes were over Chiang's long-term aims, the Korean government in exile had no choice but to nail their flag to the GMD mast. As the Chinese government moved westward, pursued by Japanese forces, the Korean leaders moved with them, ending up in Chongqing. All of their activities were closely coordinated with the GMD, and Kim Ku, who now headed the exile group, proclaimed, "Our 30 million Koreans will support our allies with our hearts and bodies to chase out our foes."[33] The armed forces of the provisional government agreed to answer directly to the Supreme Military Affairs Committee of the Guomindang. Still, Chiang doubted the efficiency of his Korean allies, seeing the government in exile as hopelessly divided—one observer claimed that the Korean leadership contained "more factions than the number of chairs in the building they were renting."[34] But their presence in Chongqing provided the Generalissimo, as Chiang now styled himself, the opportunity to represent Korea internationally, as he did when he first met his wartime allies US president Franklin Roosevelt and British prime minister Winston Churchill in Cairo in 1943. Chiang stressed the need for Korean independence after the war, though he had messaged Roosevelt before the conference that the country would be best off, at least for some time, as a "semi-independent [state] under American and Chinese tutelage."[35] Roosevelt concluded that "there was no doubt that China had wide aspirations which included the re-occupation of Manchuria and Korea."[36] The US president's own preference was for an international trusteeship with Soviet participation, a solution that Chiang was very eager to avoid. The final communique simply stated that the three countries agreed "that in due course Korea shall become free and independent."

Chiang Kai-shek's concern about Soviet influence over Korea was exacerbated by his increasing fears that Chinese and Korean Communists would have improved their positions significantly as the war came to an end. To Chiang, Asian Communists were but tools of Soviet leader Joseph Stalin and therefore out to undo the great recreation of a China-centered region that he had in mind after Japan's defeat. While Chiang's forces had borne the brunt of the fighting against Japan, Communist influence had increased significantly in northern China, including behind both Japanese and GMD lines. Lacking in international recognition and significantly outgunned by the government forces, the CCP was biding its time. Their undisputed leader, Mao Zedong, believed—as Lenin had in 1917—that the end of great wars made for unprecedented opportunities for revolutionary action. And while Japan was still expanding, Mao hoped for a Soviet entry into the war that would turn the tables both on the Japanese and the Guomindang.[37]

While preparing for postwar opportunities, the CCP had their own challenges with Koreans in the Communist ranks. The Comintern prior to 1936 had criticized Korean Communists for excessive nationalism, and then during the war it turned around and exalted "united front" ideals. The CCP followed the Comintern line, also with regard to Korea. So when Korean Communists prior to 1936 were attacked for claiming that their country was uniquely ancient as a nation, later they were censured for not understanding that the struggle was for national liberation, not social revolution. Not surprisingly, the Comintern twists increased factionalism among Korean Communists, both in China, where they were CCP members, and in the Soviet Union. Although many Koreans served with the CCP forces in north China, the Communists had no plans to expand their operations into Korea. The Korean Communists were told that their task was the liberation of China as a step toward the liberation of their homeland, just like their comrades in the USSR were told that they served the Red Army first.

In August 1945, after the United States had attacked Japanese cities with atomic bombs, Stalin concluded that the war was ending and that it was time for the Soviet Union to get its part of the spoils. While negotiating with the GMD for a bilateral agreement, which would give the USSR a prominent position in Manchuria, the Soviet leader also inquired as to China's position on Korea. "Stalin: Should Korea be independent or do you have other plan? Soong [Song Ziwen, China's foreign minister]: I don't think Korea can be independent now. Stalin: But in long run. Soong: Yes. . . . Stalin: Has China intention to annex Korea? Soong: None whatever. People different, separate history. Stalin: But it was part of China. Soong: Yes, but we don't want Korea."[38] On August 9, while Stalin was still negotiating with the Chinese, the Red Army attacked the Japanese forces in Manchuria and in Korea. Overstretched and outgunned, the Japanese folded fast. On August 24, nine days after Japan had formally capitulated, the Soviets reached Pyongyang. They had already agreed on zones of operation with the Americans, setting the dividing line at the 38th parallel in Korea. The division was supposed to be temporary, but the victorious powers had no agreement on what would happen in Korea after the collapse of Japan, just a vague wording about "trusteeship."

For Chinese and Koreans the Soviet entry into the war and the Japanese capitulation set off an intense race for power. The GMD tried to send its forces into Manchuria first, but, except for the cities, the CCP mainly beat them to it, because it was easier to get into the region from their bases in northern China.

The Soviets had gotten the deal they wanted with the GMD as the war ended, and ordered the Chinese Communists to negotiate with their enemies. Although Mao Zedong did not like the idea, he had little choice but to play along. Likewise, the Americans wanted Chiang to find a negotiated solution and avoid a civil war in China. The Chinese parties at first obsessed about power in China and had little time for Korea or other parts of the region.

Korean leaders in exile were, understandably, raring to go back to their home country. But neither China, nor the United States, nor the Soviets were at first keen to send them back. The Chinese wanted transport resources used in China, and the two occupying powers wanted to create order in their zones before Korean leaders could get in the way. The Korean Provisional Government (KPG) under Kim Ku was stuck in China until November 1945. In the United States, Syngman Rhee was deeply distrusted by the US State Department for having accused the Americans of making a secret deal at Yalta to turn Korea over to the Soviets. They tried to delay his return, but the irrepressible Rhee came to Seoul in mid-October after gaining support from the US Office of Strategic Services (OSS) and the US military. In the north, the Soviets had already brought in Kim Il-sung in August, but that was because they believed that he, as a Red Army officer, could be trusted to help implement Soviet policies.

In Manchuria, the CCP and GMD adopted opposite policies with regard to the Koreans who resided there. The CCP, through its Korean officers, told the Koreans that they would protect them if they chose to stay, and, as a result, gained much support from Korean residents. The GMD, at least at first, chose to regard the Koreans as colonizers sent in by the Japanese. Although a number of leading Korean members of the CCP went to northern Korea in the autumn of 1945, most stayed in Manchuria and formed new fighting units for the CCP. When a full-scale civil war between the CCP and the GMD broke out over control of Manchuria in mid-1946 after the Soviet withdrawal from China, the CCP's Korean troops provided crucial advantages for the party. So did the proximity with northern Korea, where Kim Il-sung had become the head of a ruling Provisional People's Committee of North Korea in early 1946. With Soviet acceptance, CCP forces could move across Korean territory in their battles with the Chinese government. They also received weapons, supplies, and medical care in Korea. By late 1946, young men in north Korea were recruited to fight for the Communists in Manchuria.

Meanwhile, political infighting increased in Seoul, despite US attempts to keep control. Syngman Rhee quit "the People's Republic," which had never achieved much anyway. Instead he traveled around southern Korea to build anti-Communist organizations aimed at reunifying the country, first and foremost the Headquarters for National Unification, headed by himself and Kim Ku. He continued to criticize the Americans for being committed to a trusteeship and for attempting to cooperate with the Soviets. In spite of Rhee's poor personal relations with many American leaders, the US military in early 1946 invited him to head the Representative Democratic Council of South Korea, which it intended as an advisory body, but which Rhee saw as a Korean proto-government. He pushed for the setting up of a de facto Korean government in Seoul as soon as possible, with the result that the US military administration attempted to sideline him and find moderate Koreans to cooperate with. After President Truman announced a more anti-Communist policy in the March 1947 Truman Doctrine, Rhee responded in a letter to the US president, "In taking this courageous stand against communism, please instruct the American military authorities in Korea to follow your policy and abandon their efforts to bring about coalition and cooperation between nationalists and communists."[39]

As the Cold War intensified, the United States became more willing to accept Rhee's plans for elections in the south, even if they knew that it would mean a division of the country. For Rhee, unity was at this stage less important than power. He believed that with a sovereign government in place in Seoul, it would be possible to reunify the country when the Soviet forces left the north. The Chinese government agreed. When Kim Ku and others opposed the setting up of a south Korean separate state, the Chinese representative in Seoul attempted to force Kim to cooperate with Rhee, telling him that if he did not cooperate, he would be regarded as a defector, in spite of his long years as the main Korean leader in China. "If you believe in Communism and mean to subscribe to it," said the GMD's man in Korea, "please say so. And we shall part political enemies never to see each other again."[40] Chiang Kai-shek's message to the Koreans was that the US forces would soon be gone, and that they must work together and with China against Soviet control.

In 1948 three series of events took place that would define the relationship between China and Korea up to today. After elections in the south in May, a Republic of Korea (ROK) was set up in Seoul in August, followed by the Democratic People's Republic of Korea (DPRK) in Pyongyang in September. And on the battlefields of northern China, the tide of war turned against the Guomindang. By the end of the year Manchuria was under Communist control, and resistance to the CCP was collapsing elsewhere in the country. A new Northeast Asia was being created, with two Korean states and a Communist China. For those who had lived through the history of the region since the rise of Japan and the fall of the Qing, this was an almost unbelievable set of events, both because of their roots and their consequences. All of a sudden the Soviet Union seemed to be the predominant power. And the ideological split among Korean exiles had helped produce two rival states, each the deadly enemy of the other.

Both Korean states wanted support from their superpower sponsors to reunify the country by force. Syngman Rhee—who had come to power in South Korea in the summer of 1948 after disputed elections—had proclaimed that Korea's "position is different from that of China. We have no Communist problem in Korea. If foreign powers do not create one now we will have no civil war between the Nationalists and Communists."[41] But events in South Korea belied his words. The Americans had been putting down a number of strikes and protests inspired, at least in part, by the Communist Party. On Cheju Island there broke out a veritable rebellion against the ROK, led by local Communists and other left-wingers. It was crushed by troops loyal to Syngman Rhee. At least 15,000 people were killed.

In the north, the Korean Communists, now calling themselves the Korean Workers' Party, quickly solidified their power with Soviet assistance. Radical and comprehensive land reform was carried out, effectively redistributing land not only from the Japanese and their collaborators but from all large farms to the peasants.[42] The Soviets, who had first tried to dismantle Japanese plants in northern Korea and transport them to the USSR as war booty, gave up on that policy in the fall of 1946, and transferred the factories and mines to the embryonic North Korean state. Given the greater industrialization in the north, and the initial success of the land reform, the economy there began to turn in 1948–1949, more quickly than that in the south. From a Chinese Communist perspective, North Korea was, with Soviet assistance, in the process of becoming a successful Asian socialist regime.[43]

Already before the People's Republic of China (PRC) was declared in Beijing on October 1, 1949, the Chinese Communists had been thinking about how to organize the relationship between their new state and other socialist states in Asia. The Soviet Union was at the center of the global socialist camp, Mao Zedong thought. The Soviets and their leader, Stalin, set the overall strategy and direction for all Communist parties and the states they created. But Moscow was far away and, as the history of the Chinese Communist Party had shown, not always au courant with events in Asia. The CCP could fill the role as a center for Communist activities in Asia and help guide revolutions in other countries. For Mao, this position was a useful compromise between the internationalism of the Chinese revolution and the centrality of China in his worldview. China was backward and weak, as Mao Zedong saw it. But it had revolutionary experience and would, with the help of the Soviet Union, become a modern Communist state rather quickly. As it refashioned itself, the PRC had a duty to help others who wanted to carry out revolution, and especially countries close to China that had been the victims of imperialist aggression, such as Korea and Vietnam.

But the CCP leadership first had to put its own house in order. The Communist conquest of China progressed slowly in late 1949 and early 1950. Xinjiang, Tibet, and the southwest were only gradually brought under PRC control. Taiwan, where Chiang Kai-shek's government had taken refuge, was at least temporarily out of reach, because the CCP armies had no amphibious capabilities. When, right after the proclamation of the PRC, Mao Zedong went to Moscow to see Stalin—Mao's first foreign trip ever—the Chinese focus was on military support to reunify the country, a long-term security alliance to protect China from imperialist attacks, and development assistance. Mao wanted to help train and supply the Vietnamese Communists who fought against France, because their battles were acute. But in the CCP's view, the unification of Korea would have to wait. Already in May 1949 Mao had told Kim Il-sung's emissaries that "in the early 1950s, if the international situation becomes favorable to North Korea's attack on the South, then actions can be taken." He was even more straightforward in conversations with Stalin. "China needs a period of 3–5 years of peace," Mao said, "in order to return China's economy to prewar levels and to stabilise the country in general."[44]

In the late 1940s, for most Koreans, the idea of a long-term division of their country was almost unimaginable. Korea had suffered for over a generation under Japanese control. Nationalism was on the rise all over the country. Now Korea would take its place among modern nations. But the question of what kind of Korea this nation would be kept the country divided. Compromise between the two main factions of Korean nationalists— Syngman Rhee's traditionalists and Kim Il-sung's Communists—seemed next to impossible. Those who tried to keep the country united often got in harm's way. Kim Ku was assassinated in June 1949. Thousands of people in the south who agitated for negotiations were killed or imprisoned, and there were casualties in the fighting between ROK forces and Communist guerrillas. In the north, landowners, businesspeople, and religious leaders were arrested or executed. Almost one and a half million people fled south because they feared Communism or religious persecution.[45] Both Rhee and Kim appealed to their foreign patrons for increased military assistance, so they could reunify their country. But even though both Washington and Moscow suspected that a Korean civil war was brewing, they were not keen on playing a role in such a war. By the summer of 1949 both powers had withdrawn the bulk of their forces from Korea, in spite reports from their intelligence agencies that the Korean governments were preparing attacks against each other.

Syngman Rhee hoped that the US withdrawal and the rapid buildup of his own forces would soon tip the balance of power toward South Korea. Even though he had no concrete plans for an immediate general offensive against the north, he strongly believed that time was on his side. So, in ways that became critical, did the North Korean leaders and their Soviet advisers in Pyongyang. Kim Il-sung appealed repeatedly for Stalin's support in an attack on the south, claiming that the North Korean advantage was greater now than what it would be in the future, when the southern guerrillas had been crushed and the region, with US assistance, had recovered economically and militarily. At first Stalin turned him down, not least because of the on-going Chinese civil war. But in January 1950 Stalin turned around, because of the CCP's military victory and because he wanted to retaliate for perceived Western provocations in Europe and Japan. The Soviet leader indicated that he would support an armed reunification of Korea. But only if the Chinese Communists were willing to support it, too.

Armed with Stalin's acceptance, Kim Il-sung in May 1950 made his way to Beijing to ask for China's support. For a whole host of reasons, Mao Zedong could not turn him down. It would have meant challenging Stalin's decision. It would also have meant disregarding North Korean support for the CCP's own campaign to reunify China by force. But perhaps most importantly, it would have implied that the Communists' New China did not intend to reestablish the close links with Korea that had been broken by the rise of Japan. In spite of the DPRK having been set up before the PRC, the Chinese leader often referred to the Korean Communists as "younger brothers." To keep that family order intact, China could not refuse to go along with Kim's plans. Even though Mao was clear that practical support for the Korean operation would have to be limited, Kim got what he was looking for. In return, he promised both the Soviets and the Chinese that unity would be achieved quickly after the military takeover, so that US forces would not have time to intervene.

The Korean War

Throughout the late spring and early summer of 1950 the North Koreans and their Soviet advisers prepared the attack on the south. The Chinese Communists were kept informed, but only in broad strokes. The offensive across the 38th parallel began at dawn on June 25, 1950. Seoul fell on June 28. Over the next few days the South Korean army collapsed, and the North Korean offensive continued at great speed. Both sides summarily executed their political opponents wherever they could put their hands on them. By mid-July Kim Il-sung believed the war would be over within weeks. The Chinese were doubtful. Although they were disposed to believe the verdicts of their Soviet comrades, they regarded Kim as a swaggering upstart and feared an American intervention, supported by Japan.[46]

At first it seemed as if Kim Il-sung was right. By late August the ROK and their US advisers were contained in a small area around Busan, under constant artillery fire and lacking supplies. But the North Korean forces were also running out of matériel and provisions. They paused before the final push against Busan. Elsewhere in the country they were busy rounding up their enemies and setting up new political organizations patterned on those in the north. The Chinese leaders started to move troops to the border, mainly as a precaution if Kim's predictions failed, but also to show the Soviets that the CCP was an internationalist party that would help the Communist cause if needed.

The US government, under Harry S. Truman's administration, had from the beginning little doubt that the United States must strike back in Korea. For Truman this was first and foremost about the Cold War with the Soviet Union. Already under fire at home for not having prevented the Communist takeover of China, Truman was not going to accept another Soviet-inspired Communist offensive without reacting strongly. The planning for a US intervention began immediately, much helped by the continued US military presence in Japan. On September 15, General Douglas MacArthur's forces landed at Inchon near Seoul. Within days the US troops had cut the country in half, trapping large numbers of North Korean units in the south, while crossing the 38th parallel, moving north. Pyongyang fell October 19, and on October 26 South Korean forces reached the eastern part of the Chinese border. The rapidity of the offensive was much due to US air superiority, which devastated North Korean defenses and landed paratroopers behind enemy lines.

The CCP government had a choice to make. Its troops were already in the northeast, ready to cross into Korea. But the Chinese leaders were aware of the power and rapidity of the US-led offensive—and the fact that Truman, because the Soviet had boycotted the UN Security Council, could designate its offensive a UN operation and call on the support of other countries. New China had just been established and could not fight against the world. Some CCP leaders opposed a Chinese intervention because it could derail the rebuilding of China. But others claimed that a foreign army on China's border would be an existential threat against their new regime. As in the past, Korea was the entry point for China. The United States, which had supported the GMD during the civil war, was their enemy and

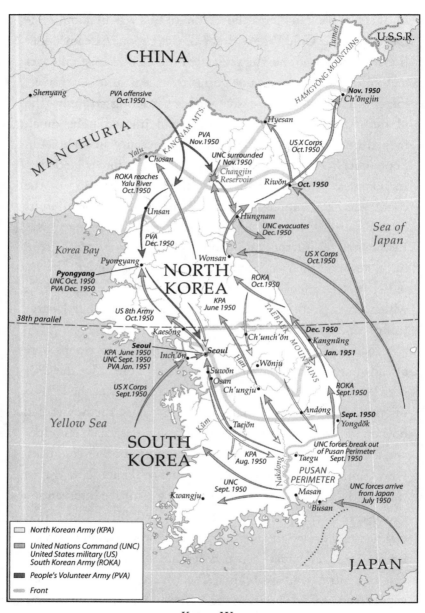

MAP 2.2 Korean War, 1950–1951

would use the Communists' humiliation in Korea to put pressure on China as well, helped by Japan and the GMD remnants on Taiwan and elsewhere.

For Mao Zedong—who in 1950 was the undisputed leader of the CCP—ideology, history, and security seem to have mattered in equal amounts. Mao put more emphasis on the ideological cohesion within the socialist camp than did many of his comrades. The CCP had a duty to assist the Korean comrades. Besides, they had assisted the CCP in the past, and Korea and China were closely related countries. Also, on October 1, Stalin had personally asked Mao to move divisions toward the 38th parallel. Mao sensed that Stalin was out to test his and the CCP's dedication to the Communist cause. Still, the Chinese leader hesitated to give the order. At the Politburo meeting on October 2, there was a clear majority against intervention. It took almost two weeks of discussions in the Politburo and with the Soviets before Mao finally decided to intervene. Chinese forces, which the CCP had styled "the Chinese People's Voluntary Army," began crossing into Korea on October 19.

On October 25 the Chinese forces attacked on a broad front in northern Korea. The scale of the attack came as a complete surprise to the US and South Korean forces, which were forced to retreat with heavy losses. Pyongyang fell in early December and Seoul in early January 1951. By spring the Chinese and North Koreans had been driven back north of Seoul, in part because of a regrouping of the US forces and in part because of extraordinarily heavy use of air power. More US bombs were dropped on North Korea during the war than the total amount used in the Pacific War. By the summer of 1951 it became increasingly clear that ground operations had stalemated, roughly where the division line had been prior to the North Korean attack. The war dragged on for another two futile years because neither the great powers nor the Korean sides could agree to a cease-fire. When it ended in July 1953—mainly because Stalin, who had opposed negotiations, died suddenly—more than two and a half million Koreans, around 13 percent of the population, had been killed or wounded in the war.

After all the disasters Korea had experienced in the twentieth century, this war was by far the worst. In destruction it can only be compared with the Imjin War of the late sixteenth century. All cities and towns in Korea were destroyed. In Seoul, which had changed hands four times in heavy fighting, thousands of people were living in rubble. Reporters described families scavenging for food and living under tarpaulins that provided flimsy shelter between whatever two walls might still be standing. In the north, US bombs—explosive, incendiary, napalm—had destroyed not only urban areas but much of the countryside as well. At least five million Koreans were refugees in their own country, in addition to the millions who had been displaced in their own city or region. There were nearly two million orphans. As regular societies, both North and South Korea had ceased existing.

The outcome also kept Korea divided. In the north, Kim Il-sung had returned to power, in spite of the dreadful mistakes he had made in executing the war. His Soviet backers protected him, and the Chinese—who had done most of the fighting—did not have their own candidate to put in his place. In the south, Syngman Rhee also survived, in spite of plentiful US misgivings. According to the new US president, Dwight D. Eisenhower, US policy on Rhee had to be "We still love you, you s.o.b."[47] Psychologically the war did much to cement the division of the country. People in the north felt that terrible things had happened to them because of the traitors in the south. And southerners mourned relatives and friends lost as a consequence of the North's attack and the Chinese they had brought into the country. Given the fierceness and cruelty of the fighting among Koreans, it would not have been easy to put the country together again, even if international politics had allowed for it.

The Korean War was also a disaster for China. Not only did it suffer 800,000 military casualties, more than any other party to the war, but the domestic development the country so badly needed was set back by several years. The war also radicalized CCP policies, so that campaigns against real or perceived enemies intensified and became more brutal and long-lasting. Because the United States moved to protect Chiang Kai-shek's rump regime on Taiwan, reunification was out of the question. Some Chinese who were in the know also felt that it had not really been China's war. It was started by a young Korean leader without any regard for China's interests, but with Stalin's blessing. And, in the view of many Chinese leaders, it was China that had to mop up the pieces and pay the price for defending Korea.

Although some Chinese were worried by the war's outcome, Mao Zedong definitely did not share their view. To him, the war was part of the big project for China's renovation. After having lost every war it had engaged in for a hundred years, China had now stood up to the most powerful country on earth and fought it to a standstill. And in Mao's view the war also had other advantages. It had cemented the Sino-Soviet security alliance and convinced the Soviets that China was a powerful socialist state. It protected the Chinese border in the northeast. And it had allowed the CCP to adopt a more sweeping approach to transforming Chinese society, an approach that the Chairman had very much sympathized with in the first place. Not having recovered Taiwan rankled. But that loss—always imagined as temporary—paled in comparison with China's achievements during the war, at least in Mao's view.

Although Chinese commanders were shocked by the North Korean military collapse when they first arrived, the practical cooperation between the two sides developed reasonably well during the war. According to most accounts, the Chinese Communists behaved better toward the civilian population than any other foreign army that had ever fought in Korea. North Korean officers complained about their Chinese allies' overbearing attitude, and Kim Il-sung resented being treated like a child by the battle-hardened People's Liberation Army (PLA) generals. But the relationship held up: the Koreans knew that they were militarily dependent on the PLA, and Mao Zedong was willing, right up to the end of the war, to provide at least lip service to the strategic aim of unifying Korea. After the spring of 1951, when his commanders reported that they did not see much chance for further advances, Mao told them that they "should understand that the Korean problem cannot be settled without experiencing a serious struggle, without eliminating all or at least most of the puppet forces, and without eliminating at least 40,000 or 50,000 more of the American and British forces."[48] In spite of their ideological emphasis on self-sufficiency, the Korean Communists knew that without China's assistance they would not have survived.

The Korean War created the framework for China-Korea relations for the rest of the twentieth century, and in some respects into the twenty-first. North Korea kept its close relations with the Soviet Union, and was strategically dependent on Chinese support. South Korea was equally dependent on the United States, and Syngman Rhee was determined to be seen as the Americans' best friend in Asia, even if he chafed under US advice and restraints. Diplomatically, North Korea was recognized only by the Communist countries, and South Korea by the main Western countries. China had no contact with South Korea, and in the minds of many Chinese, North Korea became the real Korea, "their" Korea. The Koreans' choice of names for their competing republics played a role in this mental separation: North Korea called its state Chosŏn minjujuŭi inmin konghwaguk—literally, the Democratic People's Republic of Chosŏn. And the South Koreans Taehan minguk—the Republic of Great Han (Korea). In Chinese, North Korea became Chaoxian and South Korea Hanguo.

Names matter, but probably less than freedom from want and starvation. The rebuilding of the two Koreas after the war was arduous. The fighting had reduced the country to ruins and the people to destitution. At first, progress was slow, especially in the South. In North Korea, where the economy was entirely run by the state, assistance from the socialist countries could be put to good use within the regime's development plans. In many ways the rebuilding of the DPRK was a joint Communist project, to which the USSR was the biggest contributor. South Korea also received significant foreign assistance, first and foremost from the United States. But continued political tension and lack of economic integration and coordination meant low growth rates up to the early 1960s. Land reform in the South did help alleviate poverty and created a large number of privately owned farms, which increased the food supply and, eventually, access to credit through bank savings.

The political picture was not entirely rosy in the North, either. After the war, Kim Il-sung set himself up as a Korean version of Stalin or Mao, centralizing power and persecuting enemies, real or imagined. Those who had links with Kim from his guerrilla days were promoted, and others, who had served in China or in the underground resistance, were sidelined. Kim's purges and his willful resistance to Chinese or Soviet political advice put him in a perilous position when the new Soviet leader, Nikita Khrushchev, embarked on his de-Stalinization strategy in 1956. Khrushchev invited Kim to Moscow, where he was kept for six weeks and berated for his political stubbornness. In Pyongyang, Kim's political rivals prepared to depose him on his return. After promising the Soviets that he would make amends, Kim returned to Korea, where he turned on his rivals and defeated them. The Chinese leaders, who had never warmed to Kim personally, agreed to send Marshal Peng Dehuai, the commander of the Chinese forces in the Korean War, to Pyongyang alongside Soviet delegates to force Kim to settle with his opponents. Again Kim assured them that he would change his ways. But as soon as the delegation left, Kim's opponents found themselves in prison or worse. The following year Kim unleashed a massive purge against all Korean Communist leaders but his own close supporters. Thousands were executed. Some fled to China or the Soviet Union.[49]

Meanwhile, the political turmoil continued in South Korea. Against the will of the National Assembly, Syngman Rhee instituted direct elections for president, which he won handily. He abolished term limits so he could run again in 1956. After his reelection, he arrested the heads of the main opposition party. Its leader, Cho Pong-am, was executed in 1959, having been falsely accused of spying for the North. In March 1960 Rhee was again returned to office, in an obviously rigged election. This time widespread protests broke out, especially among students. A month later, with massive demonstrations rocking the country, Rhee ordered the army to fire on student protesters in Seoul, and 180 were killed. When professors and community leaders joined the student protests, the army unit commanded to use force against them refused. The Eisenhower administration asked the US embassy to prepare for "a broadly based Korean administration dedicated to Free World principles and security objectives and to effective operation [of a] genuinely democratic political system capable of maintaining popular support."[50] On April 26, 1960, Syngman Rhee resigned and later went into exile in Hawaii. More than any other person, Rhee had been the architect of modern Korean nationalism. But in his view, ordinary Koreans did not strongly enough support the high ideals of the nation. They needed strong leadership in order to rededicate themselves to Korean traditions and endeavors. Young Koreans, though, had had enough of the old man's visions, which did not show them a better future ahead.

China and Korea after the Korean War

By the late 1950s North Korea was developing into a socialist state very similar to the Soviet Union and the less developed countries of Eastern Europe. Early Japanese industrialization had given it a head start over both China and South Korea. Learning from the Soviets had created a planned economy that functioned well, at least compared with anything Korea had seen in the past. With its emphasis on ideological rectitude and state power, North Korea was a not unlikely successor to Chosŏn, though built on a different mix of ideas. Kim Il-sung launched the concept of *Chuch'e,* later translated as "self-reliance," as his contribution to Marxist philosophy.[51] It was in part an attempt to justify his increasingly personalized dictatorship, but also carried echoes of Chosŏn-style reverence for the king, mixed with Stalinist totalitarian ideas and Christian and Buddhist millenarian visions. *Chuch'e* postulates a united nation, in a hierarchical form reminiscent of Confucianism, with the party and the leader on top. This nation will be independent and self-reliant. There is nothing, Kim argued, that the Korean nation cannot achieve if it believes in its own strength and does not dance to someone else's tune. All a bit rich, coming from a leadership that was entirely dependent on Soviet and Chinese support for its survival, but it helped solidify party rule and Kim's own position inside North Korea.

Even so, given his poor relations with the Communist great powers, it is unlikely that Kim Il-sung would have survived politically if it had not been for the Sino-Soviet split from 1959 on. As Mao Zedong became increasingly dissatisfied with the slow pace of Soviet-style transformation of the Chinese economy and society, he insisted on a series of intense campaigns to propel China forward. The first of these was the Great Leap Forward, starting in 1958. Mao also chafed under Soviet advice, which he regarded as arrogant and disrespectful, and suspected the Soviets of wanting to control China's foreign affairs. As the Great Leap policies turned into an economic disaster, Mao feared that the Soviets, and the Chinese who were close to them, would use the failure to attack him. Mao therefore organized a strategy of criticizing Khrushchev and other Soviet leaders for insufficient dedication to the Communist cause. By 1960 it was clear that the two Communist giant states were heading for some kind of clash.

With Moscow and Beijing at loggerheads, Kim was out of the woods regarding any concerted attempt to remove him as a Stalinist relic. But he now faced the opposite challenge, fearing that the Sino-Soviet split could weaken international Communism's dedication to defend North Korea. At first Kim tried to tread water, appealing for socialist unity, then eventually realized that if he were forced to take sides, Soviet accusations against Mao for perpetuating Stalinist ideas in China could also be turned against him. Gratitude for China's support during the war and a sense of Asian solidarity may also have made him lean toward the Chinese side. By 1963 North Korea seemed to be entirely in the Chinese camp, unleashing verbal broadsides against the Soviet Union, accusing it of great-power chauvinism and of having "given up its anti-imperialist struggle."[52] Mao read this as meaning that North Korea helped confirm his position as leader of the Asian revolution and China's resumption of centrality within the region.

But the Chinese had misjudged the sensitivities of Korean nationalism. As China drifted toward the Cultural Revolution in the mid-1960s, the North Korean leadership sensed that China was attempting to subsume Korea's own revolutionary experience under that of Mao Zedong and the CCP. Kim Il-sung had little sympathy for or understanding of the Cultural Revolution; he believed in order, regulation, and gradual progress, and it seemed that what was happening in China was a negation of these values. "The leaders of the KWP [Korean Workers' Party] speak of the so-called 'Great Cultural Revolution' as a 'great madness, having nothing in common with either culture or a revolution,'" reported the Soviet embassy in Pyongyang gleefully.[53] When Cultural Revolution activists among the Chinese in North Korea started rallying in favor of events at home, they were deported by the North Koreans. "The behavior of the Chinese was not compatible with the principles of proletarian internationalism and one should instead declare it a bourgeois nationalist action," Kim Il-sung told the Cubans. "Mao Zedong has made twice as many mistakes as Khrushchev did."[54]

With China increasingly consumed by the Cultural Revolution, its relations with North Korea deteriorated fast. In Beijing and other Chinese cities, Red Guards shouted slogans denouncing Kim Il-sung as a revisionist and a follower of "Khrushchev's line." In Pyongyang, the North Koreans responded by restricting access to the Chinese embassy. In Manchuria, Red Guards rounded up more than 10,000 Koreans, accusing them of being spies for North Korea; many of these ended up in prison camps and a few were executed. In addition, the Chinese put up loudspeakers along the Korean border, sending out messages condemning Soviet and Korean revisionism. In 1968 and 1969 there were several small-scale military clashes along the border. Publicly, the North Koreans always refrained from criticizing China, but for the KWP the Chinese actions were powerful reminders of the need for unity and independence. If anything, the Cultural Revolution era in China strengthened Kim Il-sung's hold on power in North Korea.

There is no indication that Kim ever gave up the idea of re-unifying the country by force. He was inspired by the Communist war for reunification in Vietnam and by the whole era of decolonization in the 1960s. To Kim Il-sung, increasingly, Korean unification was a matter of decolonization. He saw the United States, supported by Japan, as occupiers of the southern half of Korea and his regime as representing genuine Korean nationalism. While the Sino-Soviet split made a new attack on the South less feasible, Kim authorized a series of actions to draw attention to his cause. In 1968 the North Koreans took over a US Navy spy ship that they claimed had entered their territorial waters. At about the same time, a group of North Korean commandos tried to kill the South Korean president in his residence in Seoul. Irrespective of the trouble in the socialist camp, the North Koreans were determined not to be ignored.

The biggest obstacle for North Korea's reunification schemes was the economic development that had started in the South in the 1960s. The military dictatorship that had taken power in the early part of the decade, with US support, had advanced an economic strategy that mobilized domestic resources and American assistance to create an increasingly successful export economy. By 1970 the South Korean military leader Park Chung-hee had presided over a period of growth that had brought the South Korean per capita GDP almost up to North Korean levels. By 1980 it would be twice as large, and 1990 four times as large (today it is more than ten times North Korea's per capita levels). The South Korean economic miracle changed most assumptions about the viability of the Republic of Korea. Even its allies were surprised how quickly the South Korean economy grew. And although there was great income inequality, many people in the South became able to participate in its economic success by purchasing property or getting a higher level of education.[55]

In political terms, South Korea remained a dictatorship under General Park Chung-hee.[56] Park had grown up during the Japanese occupation and was trained as a military officer in Japan. He later served under Japanese leadership in the Manchukuo army during World War II. Park's vision of Korea's development was influenced by the lessons he had drawn from Japan. He wanted rapid industrialization under strong state leadership, with mobilization of all the country's resources through interaction between the government and private businesses. Park was a nationalist who believed that Korea should be reunified under his anti-Communist regime, but that it was unlikely to happen during the Cold War, since North Korea, in spite of Communist quarrels, was protected by China and the Soviet Union. His priority, therefore, was economic development in South Korea, the alliance with the United States (Park sent Korean forces to fight in Vietnam), and the crushing of domestic dissent, which he viewed as inspired by the North and therefore treasonous. Park stressed Korea's domestic culture; he strictly limited the use of Chinese script for official purposes, just like the North Koreans had done a decade earlier.[57]

Frightened by what he saw as the rapid rise of the Soviet Union, Mao Zedong in the early 1970s sought to achieve some form of accommodation with the United States. After US president Richard Nixon visited Beijing in 1972, North Korea was quick to tack farther toward the Soviets, without ever giving up its links with China. All through the 1970s and 1980s, Kim Il-sung elaborately played Moscow and Beijing against each other to North Korea's advantage, securing his regime but also acquiring the funding and technology necessary to keep the slowing North Korean economy going. Kim was also quick to reap the diplomatic rewards of superpower détente—the two Koreas joined the United Nations as full members and set up relations with countries all over the world. Kim was particularly eager to link up with new states in the Third World, to whom he offered North Korean expertise on security, engineering, medicine, and economic organization. In parts of Africa, North Korea supported movements of national liberation, taking care to aid some that were supported by the Soviets and some that were supported by the Chinese. Having aided Robert Mugabe's Zimbabwe African National Union before it came to power, the North Koreans provided advisers and weapons that enabled Mugabe to crush dissent in the Ndebele regions in the mid-1980s.

On the South Korean side, Park Chung-hee attempted some degree of relaxation of the relationship with the North. In May 1972 he sent high-ranking representatives to Pyongyang to talk directly with Kim Il-sung. Kim welcomed the southerners, and said that he dreamed of reunification. "Let us exclude for-eign forces. Let's not fight. Let's unite as a nation. Let's not take issue with Communism or capitalism," Kim exclaimed.[58] But the visit led to little progress. Unnerved by US détente policies and fearing a US withdrawal from Korea, Park moved to strengthen the dictatorship in the South. In 1974 a Korean-Japanese assassin, who had been in close touch with North Ko-rean agents in Japan, attempted to kill President Park, but the bullet missed and instead killed Park's wife standing next to him. Visiting China the following year, Kim Il-sung tried to claim that the victory of the Vietnamese Communists and po-litical unrest in South Korea made the timing opportune for an-other attempt to reunify Korea by force. Deng Xiaoping, who was gradually fastening his grip over Chinese foreign policy, turned him down flat. Deng had other priorities for China.

The process of economic reform and opening that Deng oversaw after Mao Zedong's death in 1976 changed China–Korea relations in fundamental ways. From the very beginning of the process, South Korean companies began working with officials and managers in China, and trade and investment began to grow, mainly indirectly and in spite of the lack of official rec-ognition between the two countries. For China, South Korea became a very important source of technology imports, and mu-tual trade quickly grew, reaching more than $1 billion by 1985. By 1990 it was $5–$6 billion, and growing faster than ever. All the leading South Korean companies had offices in Beijing, and from 1989 the Chinese government gave up on channeling South Korean trade through Hong Kong and allowed direct trade be-tween the two countries, despite diplomatic nonrecognition.

The process of economic reintegration between China and South Korea began as political instability again took hold in South Korea. On October 26, 1979, President Park Chung-hee was murdered by his own intelligence chief on the grounds of the presidential mansion in Seoul. Toward the end of his life, Park had wanted to set up full diplomatic relations with Beijing. The military strongmen who replaced him did not manage to hold the regime together. Challenged by student-led popular unrest, they agreed to free elections in 1987, and from then on South Korea has been a democracy, although one on which the largest business conglomerates have had a significant influence. The new president, Roh Tae-woo, declared his intention to normalize relations with both China and the Soviet Union, and, eventually, with North Korea as well.

As the Cold War drew to a close in the late 1980s, the strategic situation around the Korean Peninsula began to change. With the United States and the Soviet Union no longer locked in enmity, many Koreans began to hope that reunification would be possible. In a South Korea buoyed both by economic success and the recent democratic breakthrough, an increasing number of young people imagined that a reform-oriented China would help resolve Korean divisions. Many of them were angry at the long-standing US support for South Korean dictators and wanted their country to be less dependent on the United States in the future. China under reform seemed an attractive partner for South Korean ambitions, even after Deng Xiaoping crushed China's own democracy movement in 1989.

And China seemed to hold out hope that such a reorientation would be possible. In 1988 Chinese leaders supported the principles President Roh had put forward for developing peaceful relations between the two Koreas, even after it was clear that the North Koreans would reject them. Meanwhile, secret diplomacy between Beijing and Seoul, at times assisted by the Americans, nudged the recognition issue forward. In June 1990 Soviet leader Mikhail Gorbachev shocked Asia by announcing diplomatic recognition of Seoul. Driven in part by economic motives, Gorbachev also envisaged Soviet–South Korean normalization as a step to create peace in Korea. For Beijing the Soviet decision made it easier to move toward full recognition. The USSR, a Chinese official pointed out to me at the time, had opted to take the political flak from the DPRK, and he hoped that China could move in the Soviet shadow. Even so, it was the deepening economic relationship that pushed the decision forward. By the early 1990s China was already South Korea's third largest trading partner, and the Chinese were hungry for Korean investment. In August 1992 Beijing and Seoul announced that they would establish full diplomatic relations with each other.

North Korean leaders watched in disbelief as all of this was going on. The Cold War world, which had allowed North Korea to flourish according to its own style, was melting before their eyes. Reacting furiously to what they saw as Soviet betrayal in 1990, they tried to reach out to the South Koreans with a set of agreements, including an anti-nuclear treaty, but none of these went into effect. When Beijing recognized South Korea, North Korean public reaction was more sorrow than anger, even though Chinese and North Koreans had sharp exchanges in private. A main Pyongyang newspaper noted, "We should be armed with extraordinary courage for continuously advancing the march of hardships because in front of socialist revolution lies a long and precipitous road and river of flames. As historical experiences tell us, a socialism, which opens its door to the bourgeois ideology and neglected its task to inject socialist ideology to its people cannot avoid devastation."[59] North Korea, Kim Il-sung insisted, was the last, best hope for the Korean nation. And he would not give in. "That is why I frequently tell the young people that a ruined nation is as good as dead," Kim said in his memoirs. "That if they do not want to be a stateless people, they must go all out to defend the country, and that in order not to end up as slaves they must make the country more prosperous and collect even one more piece of rubble to build the defenses higher."[60]

The twentieth century had, for the most part, been a very bad time for Korea and for Sino-Korean relations. Just as Korean concepts of nation were finding their contemporary form, the country had been colonized by Japan. In the process, ancient ties with China had been broken; in the latter part of the century they were put back together in a new way. But the new Chinese state, which Koreans had to relate to, had also been transformed by nationalisms. Having inherited an empire, Chinese Communists increasingly believed that they ruled a nation-state, in which all inhabitants had to think of themselves as Chinese in one form or another. Koreans suffered from having two states on its territory, one increasingly dysfunctional. But they also had to deal with a China rising in a completely new form. The suzerain had been replaced by a highly centralized, interest-driven national state that sought new ways to subsume the region under its control.

3

China and Korea Today

Over a short period of time, leading up to the last years of the twentieth century, China and Korea had gone through remarkable transformations. China had developed from being an inward-looking society, driven by endless political campaigns during Mao Zedong's last years in power, to an expansive, market-oriented, ever-changing society in the 1990s. About the only thing that had not changed was the Communist Party's hold on power, even though that power, domestically at least, was now exercised for very different purposes than before. Korea had also ended up very different from what most people would have expected. South Korea, which had been dirt-poor and downhearted, had become one of the world's most successful economies and a fledgling, competitive democracy. North Korea, which at first seemed to have advanced more rapidly through socialist planning, fell behind and was left vulnerable by the collapse of its Soviet allies and by China's market-oriented reform process. By the 1990s, China–Korea relations were obviously entering a new phase, although it was very hard to say what the new era would look like.

The place where the most dramatic change was expected was in North Korea. Most observers, Korean and foreign, thought that the DPRK would either collapse or be forced to undertake reforms similar to those in China. The sense of North Korean weakness increased greatly when Kim Il-sung died suddenly in July 1994. He had set up the North Korean state and led it for almost half a century. Although he had—with China's grumbling acceptance—groomed his son Kim Jong-il as his successor, thereby creating the world's first dynastic Communist state, there seemed little chance that the ploy would work. The younger Kim had a reputation as a playboy with more interest in movies and (especially) actresses than in state building. In Beijing, policymakers attempted to advise the new North Korean leader on how best to follow China's reform example through working closely with Beijing. But they also seemed to position themselves to avoid blame inside the CCP in case of a North Korean collapse.

As Kim Jong-il fought to take control of the state in the mid-1990s, North Korea's economy began to spin out of control. In spite of its public ideology of self-sufficiency, North Korea had been an integral part of the Soviet-led socialist economic order, and had both imported and exported goods within that system at rates well below market prices. China's trade with North Korea had also been set at artificially low cost. With the USSR gone and with China increasingly demanding market prices for its goods, North Korea was forced to dramatically reduce imports, including food, fertilizers, and agricultural machinery. Food rationing, which had always existed, was lowered dramatically, with rural areas suffering the most. In 1994–1995, drought and floods also reduced agricultural output. Worst of all, the regime's distribution system, on which everyone depended, started to break down, so that some areas could go months without supplies of food. The result was a world-class famine, in which (according to Chinese figures) at least half a million people died. One doctor reported,

> Often children came in with minor colds or coughs or diarrhea and then suddenly they were dead. The poor diet lowered their resistance. Even if the hospital had antibiotics, their bodies were too weak. The babies were in the worst shape. Their mothers, themselves undernourished, didn't produce enough breast milk. Baby formula was non-existent and milk rare. In the past, mothers who couldn't produce enough breast milk would feed their babies a watered-down congee made from cooked rice; now most of them could not afford the rice either.[1]

Even though North Korea's people starved, it took the North Korean government a long time to appeal for foreign assistance, fearing that true accounts of the disaster would make Korea look weak. The government also feared the impact of foreign relief workers operating inside North Korea. And they feared outsiders reporting on how North Korea was really ruled. In the end they had to accept foreign offers of aid in addition to what China could give. South Korea and the United States were the biggest donors. The North Korean regime received the aid, distributed it, but tried to hide as best it could where the assistance came from. The character of the regime, including its increasing xenophobia, did not change at all.

Kim Jong-il, born in the Soviet Union during his father's exile there, was fifty-three years old when Kim Il-sung died in 1994. His father had been grooming him for succession, but the younger Kim had been an unwilling student, preferring his movie interests and girlfriends to the study of governing. When he was thrown into the top position, his health was already poor and he knew that outside of North Korea, including in China, most people looked askance at the idea of a Communist bloodline. Kim's response was to intensify the popular adoration of his father inside the country and attach himself to it. Just like the older Kim was "The Great Leader," the younger, in official propaganda, became "The Dear Leader." To Kim Jong-il and the "Kimists" who flocked to his leadership, it was precisely the bloodline that mattered: The argument for Kim Jong-il as chief was remarkably similar to Confucian concepts of principals as practiced in the idea of kingship, as in the Chosŏn. Jong-il, that argument went, had inherited his father's abilities and had been personally trained by his father. What better leader could there be, particularly in a time of great challenges? In spite of his former proclivities and disparagement from abroad, Kim Jong-il fit the North Korean image of what a leader should be.

In some ways Kim attempted to live up to his image. He began issuing new tracts on *Chuch'e* and Korean socialism, patterned on the copious works issued in the name of his father. He took an active interest in foreign relations, first and foremost with China, although it took almost six years before his first trip to the mighty neighbor was agreed to by Beijing, a clear sign of disfavor. In the wake of the hunger disaster, he allowed limited private markets to appear, but on the assumption that they would be temporary. He tolerated a significant increase in corruption among senior officials, and made certain that his own tastes in Japanese food, French wine, and Neapolitan pizza were well catered to. The regime itself became increasingly inward-looking, intolerant, and hierarchical, all centered on Kim Jong-il as supreme leader in charge of all decisions. Enemies of the regime—real or perceived—would be executed or put in prisons or re-education camps. In the year 2000, around 200,000 Koreans were in prison for political reasons (in 2019 the number is around 120,000).

North Korea had one card up its sleeve that both father and son Kim thought could be used to gain international advantages for the regime. Since the 1950s North Korean scientists and engineers had participated in joint research on nuclear issues in the Soviet Union.[2] In 1963 the Soviets had agreed to support nuclear energy development in North Korea, and the first nuclear reactor there was operational by the end of 1965. At some point in the 1980s, as the Soviets were preoccupied with events elsewhere and at home, North Korea started its own nuclear weapons program. In 1993 the International Atomic Energy Agency (IAEA) reported that North Korea seemed in violation of the Nonproliferation Treaty (NPT) that the country had signed. Later the same year the North Koreans announced their withdrawal from the NPT. This set off alarm bells in Washington and elsewhere. For the first time since the Korean War, a US administration, now under Bill Clinton, took up a North Korean invitation for talks. In October 1994, right after Kim Jong-il's accession, the two countries agreed a "Framework" to keep North Korea in the NPT. To the United States—now the world's only superpower—this seemed the kind of agreement that benign hegemons should negotiate on behalf of the world as a whole. To Kim Jong-il it must have been a godsend. It not only gave big face to his regime but also promised US aid in return for denuclearization and held out the expectation of full normalization of relations with the Americans.

But the nuclear deal between North Korea and the United States did not hold up over time. After the 1994 US election, Congress was controlled by Republicans who did not support the agreement with Pyongyang. They held back on providing funding for the oil supplies that North Korea had been promised as part of the package. They also refused to lift Korean War–era sanctions against the North. Some assistance still found its way through funds that the White House was in charge of, and other relief supplies were sent to help combat the famine. But the North Koreans were annoyed by what they saw as US noncompliance with the agreement. In return for decommissioning their Yongbyon nuclear plant, which was capable of producing weapons-grade plutonium, North Korea had been promised two light-water reactors. These were begun but never completed. The work on them came to a complete halt after George W. Bush became US president, when US intelligence reported that Pyongyang was pursuing technology for a uranium enrichment program that could produce material for nuclear weapons. After 9-11, Bush pronounced North Korea, together with Iran and Iraq, part of an "Axis of Evil," "a regime arming with missiles and weapons of mass destruction, while starving its citizens."[3]

While North Korea struggled with the outcome of the Cold War, South Korea thrived on it. Not only did reform and opening in China provide new markets for South Korean companies. Increasingly, the South Korean economy went global. Korean export products began to appear in countries the world over and, combining reasonable prices with good quality, they increased their sales rapidly. The country's GDP grew by nearly 10 percent per year from 1985 to 1995, with the GDP per capita in 1995 at around $13,000, the third highest in Asia after Japan and Singapore. The figure for China, by comparison, was $608, and for North Korea $222. The swelling South Korean middle class became accustomed to an ever-expanding level of consumption. Even the 1997 Asian financial crisis, which hit Korea badly, did not do much to dent South Korean consumer confidence. And the liberal governments of Kim Young-sam and Kim Dae-jung viewed increasing welfare for the population as a main objective, with better access to education, health, and well-paying jobs.

For Deng Xiaoping's successor, Jiang Zemin, China's Korean priorities were clear. He wanted to draw on South Korean trade, technology, and investment in order to advance the Chinese economy. To him, North Korea was at best a sideshow that served China's interests by keeping existing security agreements in place and attempting to promote Chinese-style reform from within. China contributed aid to help overcome the North Korean famine, but to a smaller degree than South Korea and the

United States. China had an interest in preventing a sudden collapse of the North Korean regime, which could lead to large flows of refugees and a reunification of Korea under US auspices. But it did not want to risk its buoyant and profitable relations with Seoul by being seen as too close to North Koreans. Jiang and his advisers saw Korean reunification not only as likely, but as forthcoming, and they wanted China to play the role of honest broker between the two Korean regimes, thereby strengthening both China's prestige and its security.

While political leaders tried to deal with strategic implications of the changes in the China–Korea relationship, Chinese businesspeople and ordinary citizens observed the fluctuations in a different way. During the 1990s and 2000s, South Korean investment in China exploded. Already in 1995, China was by far the largest recipient of Korean investment in Asia, and ten years later Korean investments there were as large as in the rest of Asia put together. Korean money and technological know-how played a significant part in China's modernization, and in some parts of the PRC, such as Shandong and Liaoning, it was predominant. Korean products became increasingly popular in China, and the number of Chinese students who studied Korean skyrocketed. None of these young people yearned to go to Pyongyang. But visiting South Korea was often their dearest hope.

The latter dreams were much connected to the extraordinary popularity of South Korean television series in China. "What Love Is All About," a Korean family drama, was broadcast on China Central Television, the major state television broadcaster, in 1997, and became the second-most viewed TV program in Chinese history. Other South Korean TV series followed, and by the mid-2000s Korean TV was by far the most popular programming in China. Millions of young Chinese identified with their Korean heroes and heroines, in part because these programs dealt with issues of love and family affairs, social betterment, the role of women, or generational gaps in ways many Chinese could identify with. Different from American or European series, and the heavily censored programs made in China itself, Korean soap operas presented a world that most Chinese could recognize in terms of values and issues, while operating in a setting that its viewers found advanced and attractive. "They are so similar to us," gushed a Chinese friend of mine who is a true aficionado of South Korean dramas.

Not surprisingly, Chinese Communist authorities started finding the attraction of Korean TV a bit threatening. In 2006 the PRC government tried to limit the number of South Korean dramas that could be imported. But the Chinese viewing audience simply turned to video-sharing websites that were much harder to regulate. Communist Party journals fumed that watching Korean series was unpatriotic, and they threatened sanctions against those that transmitted such programs illegally. One of them pointed out that the Confucian culture that so intrigued viewers of the "Korean Wave" was really China's own cultural heritage, which could be better understood through authorized and properly vetted Chinese programming.[4] Nothing helped. Even China's new president, Hu Jintao, complained privately that his many duties—including, one must assume, handling relations with Korea—prevented him from watching the latest Korean soaps.[5]

Soon the real world was to overtake that of television. Hu Jintao became China's president in 2002 just as the issues concerning the North Korean nuclear program came to the fore again after the breakdown of the Framework agreement. When the DPRK finally did withdraw from the nuclear Nonproliferation Treaty in 2003, Hu's response was to facilitate talks between all the involved parties—the two Koreas, China, the United States, Russia, and Japan—for the purpose of dismantling North Korea's nuclear program. The talks were held in Beijing and chaired by China. In many ways the Six-Party Talks marked China's return to a central position in East Asian diplomacy. The location and chairmanship of the talks indicated just who everyone else thought was in a position to prompt a solution. But Hu and his advisers had a hard time figuring out what China really wanted to stand for in the discussions about the Korean Peninsula. The Chinese wanted to bring North Korea back within the Nonproliferation Treaty. But they also wanted to stabilize the North Korean regime and provide it with international support and, if possible, security guarantees. Chinese intelligence warned the CCP leaders that Kim Jong-il now seemed determined to develop nuclear weapons of his own. But Hu believed that the survival of the North Korean regime was more important to China than tougher Chinese action against Pyongyang on the nuclear issue.

In South Korea both the liberal governments in power and the public in general believed that China would play a positive role in the nuclear talks and in attempts at creating a lasting détente-based arrangement between the two Korean states. In 2002 a record 66 percent of South Koreans viewed

China favorably. The United States, the ROK's closest ally, was only at 52 percent, and Japan, unsurprisingly, was at less than 30 percent.[6] South Korea's "Sunshine Policy," developed under President Kim Dae-jung, attempted to encourage increasing North Korean cooperation with the South by offering economic incentives. South Korea provided increasing amounts of aid to the North, and in 2000 President Kim Dae-jung traveled to Pyongyang for the first inter-Korean summit meeting with Kim Jong-il. The Chinese government supported the South Korean initiatives, while the United States, especially under the George W. Bush administration, was publicly critical. The Americans feared that South Korea would provide assistance that would make it easier for the North to resist international pressure for denuclearization.

In 2005, in part as result of the "Sunshine Policy" and Chinese pressure, the North Koreans at the Six-Party Talks agreed in principle to verifiable denuclearization of the Korean Peninsula and to abandon all nuclear weapons and nuclear programs and return to the NPT as soon as possible. Chinese foreign policy advisers were divided on how serious Kim Jong-il's new commitment was, but attempted to get the negotiations in Beijing into high gear. Meanwhile, the North Koreans, angered by US attempts to freeze Pyongyang's foreign currency accounts in overseas banks, refused to move further in the talks. Then, in October 2006, North Korea announced and carried out its first nuclear weapons test. The test, which was conducted not too far from the Chinese border, was a limited success, yielding less than 10 percent of the explosive power of the US bomb that hit Hiroshima in 1945. But what mattered was that North Korea, in violation of all its previous commitments, was now a nuclear power, defying the purposes of all other countries in the process.

The Chinese, understandably, were furious with the North Korean leaders. Even though the Chinese Communist Party Politburo had believed for some time that a test was coming, the North Korean action implied a loss of face for Beijing. Chinese leaders issued a strong public condemnation, calling the test a "flagrant and brazen" violation of international opinion and saying that China "firmly opposes" North Korea's conduct. "China strongly calls on North Korea to conform to its denuclearisation commitment, stop all the activities that might further de-stabilise the region, and [go] back to the Six Party talks."[7] In private, Chinese high-level visitors to Pyongyang were even angrier. But the North Koreans refused to budge. On one occasion a North Korean official simply read out to the visiting Chinese parts of the statement the DPRK had issued right before the test took place: "A people without reliable war deterrent are bound to meet a tragic death and the sovereignty of their country is bound to be wantonly infringed upon. This is a bitter lesson taught by the bloodshed resulting from the law of the jungle in different parts of the world. The DPRK's nuclear weapons will serve as reliable war deterrent for protecting the supreme interests of the state and the security of the Korean nation from the U.S. threat of aggression and averting a new war and firmly safeguarding peace and stability on the Korean peninsula."[8] The Chinese visitors left in a huff.[9]

Deeming the North Korean test "a clear threat to international peace and security," a UN Security Council resolution demanded, with China's support, that North Korea refrain from further nuclear or missile tests, return to the NPT, suspend all ballistic missile activities, and abandon its nuclear program in a "complete, verifiable, and irreversible" manner. It also imposed sanctions on Pyongyang until it complied fully with the demands of the UN, including bans on exports to North Korea of all heavy weaponry or spare parts for such weaponry, all WMD or missile-related technology, and some categories of luxury goods. All member states were also required to freeze financial assets related to North Korea's weapons programs. The resolution was less strong than called for by the United States and, especially, Japan. But it was still one of the most remarkable examples of post–Cold War great-power cooperation. The North Koreans were shocked and angry. They had believed that China would veto such a resolution against them. Now they proclaimed that the UN resolution constituted "an act of war" against their country.

Some Chinese leaders had been genuinely convinced that the DPRK would not test nuclear weapons because China had told them not to. These leaders were the angriest over North Korean policies. Although it implied a misreading of the history of China–Korea relations, there had been a sense that at least on matters of great importance, Kim Jong-il would necessarily follow the PRC lead. Now, with that demonstrably not the case, there was significant disagreement in Beijing on how to react. China's agreeing to the UN resolution had been the work of Hu Jintao and his closest foreign policy advisers. The Foreign Ministry urged caution to not upset China–North Korea relations further. So did some of the military chiefs and the intelligence community. In the Central Committee secretariat opinions were divided. A few hard-liners argued that the disrespect Pyongyang had shown China (and Hu personally) was so great that further pressure should be brought to bear on Kim Jong-il—for instance, through suspending Party-to-Party contacts or sharply reducing fuel deliveries. But the majority believed that such measures would accomplish little besides demonstrating China's relative impotence to the world. The lukewarm compromise was to issue statements saying that China and North Korea had normal country-to-country relations, and denying that any alliance existed between them.[10]

In 2007 China was able to drag both the North Koreans and an unwilling Bush administration back to the negotiation table. On the US side, a number of officials argued that agreeing to new negotiations would be rewarding the North Koreans for their nuclear test. Others, who in the end prevailed, said that the DPRK test had increased the stakes and that it was more important than ever to get Pyongyang to agree to denuclearization. The Chinese were, for understandable reasons, not very optimistic at first, but had underestimated the North Korean need for aid. In February 2007 Kim Jong-il agreed to shut down and seal the Yongbyon nuclear facility in return for 50,000 tons of heavy fuel oil and the complete unfreezing of North Korean assets abroad. In July 2007, IAEA inspectors confirmed that the North Korean plant had closed. But in the fall of 2007 the Americans found that the DPRK's inventory list of nuclear production facilities was inadequate and suspended aid. The Six-Party Talks did not reconvene.

Instead, in April 2009 the DPRK launched its first space satellite. The launch failed, but the attempt convinced others that North Korea was developing a technology for intercontinental ballistic missiles that could, eventually, reach the United States. In May North Korea tested its second nuclear weapon, with much greater success than in 2006. The second test in effect buried the Six-Party Talks, at least for the foreseeable future, and it was clear that the situation on the Korean Peninsula was heading in a new and more dangerous direction. While holding out the prospect of eventual denuclearization, Kim Jong-il's rhetoric became increasingly determined. "To make the whole Korean peninsula nuclear-free was the behest of the great President Kim Il-sung," he told visiting journalists in 2011. "And it is the consistent stand of the government of our Republic. The nuclear issue on the Korean peninsula arose as a result of the United States constantly threatening the sovereignty and security of our people. Sovereignty is the lifeline of a country and nation. We have possessed nuclear deterrent to protect our sovereignty from the blatant nuclear threat of the United States and its increasingly hostile policy."[11]

China's reaction to the second North Korean test was considerably less vocal than to the earlier test. The Chinese leadership said that Pyongyang's test was in "disregard for the international community's common objective," but encouraged a diplomatic solution to the problem.[12] The UN Security Council further sanctioned North Korean weapons imports and exports, but there was little agreement in other areas. After the breakdown of the Six-Party Talks, China had decided to change tack, now trying to co-opt North Korea into a Chinese-style development strategy that would make economic priorities more important and increase China's say within the regime. Most

Chinese leaders believed that the DPRK had now made it through the crises of the 1990s and early 2000s, and that a more inclusive policy could stabilize the regime further and make it more dependent on China. The Western financial crisis of 2007–2008 had convinced many Chinese that China's rise as a world power was happening more quickly than even they had expected, and that the country could therefore afford a more assertive foreign policy, at least within its own region. Hu Jintao declared 2009 the year of PRC–DPRK friendship, and Kim Jong-il visited China both in 2010 and 2011, on the latter occasion with one of his sons, Kim Jong-un.

For South Korean liberals, who had invested so much in a gradual détente with the North, the nuclear tests and the collapse of the Six-Party Talks were real disasters. South Korea had developed a number of direct links with the DPRK, including the Kaesŏng Industrial Zone, a part of North Korea about one hour's drive from Seoul, where South Korean companies invested in building factories. The products were transported to the South, and the North Korean government received the wages earned by Northerners employed there (which averaged a bit more than 6 percent of average wages in South Korea). The zone continued to operate in some form up to 2016, but never reached its full potential and was subjected to much political controversy before it closed. Tourist visits, family reunions, and humanitarian aid all came to a halt. In December 2007 South Korea elected its first conservative government in twenty years, headed by President Lee Myung-bak. Though the election of President Lee was more a consequence of, than a reason for, poor relations with North Korea, the new president quickly put in place a more confrontational policy toward the North and a closer relationship with the United States.

Over the next few years tensions between North and South continued to grow. In November 2009, ships from the two countries exchanged fire at sea. Five months later the North Koreans sank a South Korean naval corvette, the ROKS *Cheonan*, killing forty-six seamen. The attack took place well to the south of the UN-declared limit line on the Korean west coast, but in waters Pyongyang regards as disputed. As a consequence, South Korea cut all trade with the North. Then, in November 2010, the DPRK shelled the South's military positions on Yeonpyeong Island, not far from where the *Cheonan* had been sunk. Both military and civilian buildings were hit. Four people were killed and more than twenty wounded. Although the North Korean attacks are best interpreted as results of the rising tension at the demarcation lines, public reaction in the South was very strong. The number of people who thought that South Korea could do business with the North dropped precipitously. In Seoul, only thirty-five miles from the border, a higher percentage of its ten million people were more fearful of war than at any other time since polling began.

The renewed tension on the Korean Peninsula presented China with a real dilemma. Coming in the middle of Chinese attempts to pull North Korea closer to the PRC, Hu Jintao and his fellow leaders—never among the most imaginative of statesmen—believed Beijing should refrain from too much public censure of Kim Jong-il's aggression. In private, Chinese emissaries told the North Koreans that they were playing with fire. But officially Beijing refrained from commenting on either of the 2010 attacks. While the rest of the world blamed North Korea, Beijing was silent. The consequences were dire in terms of cooperation with South Korea and especially in terms of South Korean public opinion. Young South Koreans began thinking that China encouraged the North's hostility and that Beijing wanted to keep Korea divided. The number of South Koreans who regarded China favorably fell by about half from the early 2000s to the late 2010s. Even inside China, opposition to the official CCP line on North Korea started to grow, with an increasing number of online comments and remarks by public intellectuals critical of Kim Jong-il.

The main reason Chinese leaders' support of North Korea seemed so odd within China was the growth in South Korean soft power among the Chinese public. Many Chinese sincerely admired South Korea—some for its democratic reforms, but many more for its economic success and its alluring products, ranging from the much-lauded TV series and films to music, cars, electronics, and cosmetics. The "Korean Wave" in consumption habits from the early 2000s made South Korea a favored tourist destination, with the spots where popular TV series had been filmed especially favored. Korean-style cosmetic surgery became the rage among wealthy Chinese, who wanted to look like their favorite Korean music or movie stars. For most of those who admired South Korea, their views were not in any sense political, but some did ask, publicly, why China's leaders seemed to prefer the North. For the vast majority of Chinese, Korea's successes and travails were not in any way major issues. As with all foreign affairs, such issues paled in comparison with all the questions thrown up by China's own frenetic pace of development in the 2000s and 2010s. Indeed, in my experience, a large number of ordinary Chinese view South and North Korea as distinct and separate countries and have no understanding of how and why Korea was divided.[13]

In 2011 Kim Jong-il died at seventy. His fondness for cigarettes and fatty foods did little to help a man who had been in poor health since before he took over as leader. The North Korean authorities waited two days before announcing his death, a sign that the succession needed a bit of work to be implemented. It had been clear for some time that the ruler had been preparing his second son, Kim Jong-un, to take over, but the young man was only twenty-eight and had little experience in government. As a child Jong-un had attended a boarding school in Switzerland, so he at least knew a bit about the outside world. What mattered in North Korea was his parentage, and by all accounts young Kim threw himself into the role of dictator-in-training with gusto. The Chinese, who had rolled their eyes over the last succession, drew deep sighs at this one. One observer of Korean affairs in Beijing told me that it was still hard for the PRC leadership to get used to the idea of a Marxist-Leninist dynasty at work in a neighboring country.

As Kim Jong-un and his advisers worked to further solidify the Kim family's hold on North Korea, their outward actions became increasingly aggressive. In 2012 the North Koreans launched another satellite, this time successfully. The following year they carried out yet another and bigger nuclear test. Meanwhile, various missile tests were going on, and in 2017 the North Koreans launched four ballistic missiles into the Sea of Japan and tested their first intercontinental ballistic missiles

(ICBMs), which they claimed could reach the United States. By then, it is generally agreed, Pyongyang had also tested its first hydrogen bomb, with about 250 kilotons of explosive power, hundreds of times more than the early North Korean tests. Publicly, at least, it also claimed to have miniaturized its nuclear weapons so that they could be fit on long-range missiles. It was the latter developments that most alarmed the Trump administration as it came into office in early 2017, and let to its issuing a number of threatening statements against Kim Jong-un and the North Korean regime.

Xi Jinping, who became general secretary of the Chinese Communist Party as the young Kim fastened his hold on power in Pyongyang, intended to keep his predecessor's Korean policies. But the increasing assertiveness of Pyongyang's approach made that difficult. Although some of Xi's advisers argued that the outward aggression was simply a young man's attempt to show his toughness and fitness for office, Xi himself seems to have taken a dimmer view of North Korean actions. Along with many of his closest confidants, Xi wanted a more muscular Chinese foreign policy, which befitted the country's new status in international affairs. This was first and foremost true in relations with the United States and with Japan, or on territorial issues with regard to Southeast Asia or India. But it also affected North Korea, in the sense that many Beijing leaders felt that the young North Korean leader had disrespected China with his military ventures. When Kim had his own uncle, Jang Song-thaek—a man known for his closeness with some Chinese leaders—executed for disobedience in 2013, Beijing's disapproval began to be felt in earnest. China agreed to new UN sanctions against

North Korea, and China's public criticism of the country grew tougher. Meanwhile, Chinese authorities started to implement the sanctions along the Korean border in ways that went beyond anything seen before. In the summer of 2017 China dramatically cut its oil supplies to North Korea, obviously in order to show its disapproval of recent North Korean behavior.

North Korea refused to be brought to heel. Instead it started its own anti-China propaganda campaign. With the young leader praising the closeness of his relations with Beijing in public, the Pyongyang press—obviously with the leader's encouragement—went on the attack. One news outlet wrote about a certain neighboring country, saying that "this country, styling itself a big power, is dancing to the tune of the U.S., while defending its mean behavior with such excuses that it was meant not to have a negative impact on the living of the people in the DPRK, but to check its nuclear program."[14] "If the country keeps applying economic sanctions on the DPRK while dancing to the tune of someone after misjudging the will of the DPRK," intoned another one, "it may be applauded by the enemies of the DPRK, but it should get itself ready to face the catastrophic consequences in the relations with the DPRK."[15] Irrespective of the many times China had rescued the North Korean regime, relations seemed headed for the deep freeze again, and Pyongyang's statements made the CCP's top foreign policy advisers scramble for a better Chinese policy on Korea. Wang Yang, a member of the CCP Politburo's Standing Committee, told a visiting Japanese leader in December 2017 that "[North] Korea was once a country with which China had relations of friendship cemented in blood. But this is not the case now. Bilateral relations are now confrontational."[16] One prominent Chinese historian of Korea commented in public:

> If we look at North Korea and South Korea, who is a friend of China and who is an enemy? Outwardly, China and North Korea are allies, while the United States and Japan support South Korea against North Korea. That's a legacy of the Cold War. But I believe that after decades of contention and shifts in the international landscape, there's long been a fundamental transformation. My basic conclusion is judging by the current situation, North Korea is China's latent enemy and South Korea could be China's friend.[17]

One problem for Beijing was that if relations with North Korea were bad, they were not good with the South either. Not only had China's policies from the late 2000s on pushed away much of the goodwill that had existed in South Korea. But the reactions of the conservative South Korean governments to Pyongyang's warmongering had also alarmed Beijing. Park Geun-hye, the former dictator Park Chung-hee's daughter, who had been elected president in December 2012, decided to ask the United States to install new anti-missile defenses in South Korea, and the US government was keen on delivering such defensive weapons. An agreement was reached for setting up elements of the US-developed Terminal High Altitude Area Defense (THAAD) along the border with the North. The Chinese protested, choosing to believe that the weapons were part of global US efforts to devalue China's offensive capabilities against the United States. When the South Koreans refused to cancel the deployment of THAAD, China responded with punitive measures against South Korean companies and with limits to the number of Chinese tourists allowed to travel to South Korea. In a sign of what matters in Sino-Korean relations now, it also canceled several events featuring Korean pop bands and actors in China. The Chinese government's broadcast regulator banned South Korean TV shows and stopped approving South Korean online video games. The Chinese also pretended that a number of South Korean products, from air purifiers to cosmetics, had to be banned due to safety concerns. None of these measures did much to endear the CCP regime to young people in China, although they undoubtedly had negative effects for the South Korean economy.

The self-destruction of South Korea's first female president, Park Geun-hye, in a corruption and influence-peddling scandal in 2017 gave Korean liberals a chance to return to power that year, with Moon Jae-in as the new leader. President Moon came in with high hopes of improving relations with both North Korea and China, but the ongoing confrontation over nuclear weapons and missiles (not to mention THAAD) made that difficult. The way out for Moon proved an unlikely one. In August 2017, after the North Koreans had boasted publicly that they had nuclear missiles that could reach New York City, US president Donald Trump had warned Kim Jong-un that "North Korea best not make any more threats to the United States. They will be met with fire and fury like the world has never seen. He [Kim Jong-un] has been very threatening—beyond a normal statement—and, as I said, they will be met with fire, fury and, frankly, power the likes of which the world has never seen before."[18] The world seemed headed for a very dangerous nuclear crisis. But in March 2018 Trump suddenly agreed to a summit meeting with the North Korean leader, as had been suggested by President Moon. The South Koreans (and much of the world at large) could not believe their good luck. China was left sidelined by the new developments, although Kim managed to go to Beijing *twice* before the summit, both visits within the span of forty days. These were his first foreign trips after taking office seven years earlier. Kim also met twice with President Moon at the Demilitarized Zone that separate the two Koreas. The summit with Trump was set for June 2018 in Singapore. Not much was achieved at the meeting, and the follow-up summit in Hanoi in 2019 also ended without a concrete agreement. But all sides agreed, at least for the moment, that diplomacy was better than saber rattling.

Ever since the nuclear crises intensified the conflict on the Korean Peninsula, China has been making its military preparations for all eventualities. After the 2017 reorganization of China's military, the People's Liberation Army, it became abundantly clear just how much the fear of war in Korea affected Chinese military planning. The new Northern Theater Command of the PLA, which commands both China's northeast and the Shandong Peninsula across from Korea, consists of three army groups with more than 200,000 soldiers. The 79th army group, headquartered in Shenyang, would be responsible for spearheading a Chinese intervention in Korea. It is China's best-trained and best-equipped army, supported by several air force units, tank battalions, attack and supply helicopters, army and navy special units, and units of the People's Armed Police, all of which are specially trained for operations abroad, and some of which consist of detachments of Korean speakers. Both the second and third departments of China's Joint Staff Headquarters— responsible, respectively, for foreign military intelligence and cyber operations—have centers of operation in Shenyang, aimed at activities in Korea. Chinese military leaders appear convinced that they would be able to secure a buffer zone of at least fifty miles inside North Korea within hours, if ordered to do so.

Meanwhile, limited trade between China and North Korea continues, providing the Kim regime's only lifeline for economic survival and Beijing's main hope for prodding Pyongyang toward reform. Some businesspeople in Manchuria, including a few with military contacts, are getting very rich in the process. Smuggling is rampant, and Chinese machinery and consumer products are finding their way into North Korea quite easily, in spite of the sanctions. A few business leaders in China are dreaming about the North Korean economy opening up fully to Chinese trade and investments, giving them a leg up in the most underdeveloped market in Asia. So far there is little sign of that happening. Instead, North Korean state companies are refocusing on exports to China that would not be hit by sanctions, such as women's underwear, wigs, and false eyelashes. The Guomenwan border trade zone between China and North Korea, set up in the early 2010s, sits mainly unused.

Both for China and for the United States, relations with the two Koreas will increasingly be seen as part of the overall relationship between the two strongest powers in the world. The remarkable growth in China's economy has put it in a position within its region—and increasingly also globally—that the country has not seen for almost 200 years. Increasingly, all other countries in East Asia are looking to China to lead in terms of international affairs, at the same time as they fear and sometimes resent the astonishing rise in Chinese power. The increase in China's military capacity is particularly worrisome for its neighbors; China's defense spending is now higher than that of all other eastern Asian powers combined, including India and Russia (though it is still only a third of US military expenditure). After having spent a generation easing China's access to international capital and markets in order to socialize the Chinese into a US-led international order, most American leaders have now started seeing China as a global rival, and many see it as a potential enemy.

The future of the China-US relationship will therefore determine many of the parameters for developments in Korea and between Korea and China. But it is not the only determinant. North Korea's domestic situation will remain potentially unstable as long as the regime is not able to feed its people or give them hope for a better life in the future. Koreans in the north are less and less shut off from the world at large, and from their countrymen in the south. An increasing number know how other people live, and aspire to comforts that at the moment seem unattainable. This is the reason their young leader Kim Jong-un wants to turn his economy from increasing military capacity to civilian production, as when he declared at the end of 2017 that the DPRK had "finally realized the great historic cause of completing the state nuclear force."[19] But, as the Chinese often observe, Kim is also fearful of making use of economic tools that could jump-start the country's economy, dreading that any liberalization could endanger the regime itself. Meanwhile, a 2018 opinion poll found that 91 percent of South Koreans believed that China does not want Korean unification, now or ever, while support for national unity among the South Korean population itself remain high, though increasingly diverse in terms of outlook. Especially young South Koreans believe that unification should be a gradual process, driven by the Koreans themselves. They are less and less keen on allowing any foreign power, including China and the United States, a major role in determining how Koreans will unify their country.

CONCLUSION

What Can We Learn from History about China-Korea Relations?

As we have seen, Chinese and Koreans have formed close but complex bonds over the past six hundred years. In cultural terms they have been closer than most groups that speak different languages, and they have a remarkable number of beliefs, symbols, and traditions that are similar. Furthermore, both groups have been aware of these similarities through both interaction and imitation, to such a degree that it has at times been difficult to distinguish what was and is Korean from what was and is Chinese. As we have also seen, their shared history is full of admiration, but also, at times, of resentment. At the heart of the story, within the cultural and historical propinquity, is the Chosŏn and its Korean successor states' defense of their political autonomy against the empire next door.

Handling empires from the outside is always a difficult task, especially if you happen to be right next to one. Plenty of Asians, Europeans, Arabs, and Africans (not to mention native Americans or Australians) have discovered this the hard way over the past millennia. Chances are that you will be swallowed up, willingly or not. As we discussed in the first part of the book, not all empires are alike. But for imperial projects to be successful, they have to be at the center of some form of regional or global order; such orders often have led others from subservience through to subsumption. For Korea to keep some form of political independence over six hundred years is therefore no mean feat.

There are many reasons Korea was never incorporated into the empire. One is what might be termed complex sovereignty.[1] Unlike in the European Westphalian system, Asian empires and states have long recognized that total sovereignty for any country is a chimera.[2] This is especially true for smaller countries on the edge of empire. For centuries the Chosŏn state identified as a vassal of the Ming and Qing empires. Through time-honored practice, this meant that Korea governed its own affairs domestically, but was subservient to and dependent upon the empire for its defense and foreign affairs. Koreans were well aware that established conventions meant little if the empire chose to use force against them. Therefore they prepared assiduously to stand up for their independence. But neither did these conventions mean nothing. In themselves, established practices that regulated levels of incorporation and areas of sovereignty were parts of Korea's defense and of its identification as a highly civilized Confucian state. Complex sovereignty was not simply negative, in the sense that it limited what either side could do. It was also positive, providing identities for both sides that played to their strengths: the empire as benevolent and authoritative; Chosŏn as civilized, steadfast, and reliable.

Another reason for Korean separateness could perhaps be termed compound singularity, meaning how Koreans came to see themselves as distinct and sometimes, in the twentieth century especially, as unique, while recognizing cultural as well as political ties to the empire next door.[3] The establishment of separate, but connected, mythologies and histories plays an important part in this. Also, Korean elites developed sets of imagined identities, qualities of what I here have called a nation, some of which were also accepted and incorporated into their own views of Korea by Chinese rulers. Loyalty, earnestness, and determination were among these Korean qualities, according to the Chosŏn and, at least at times, according to imperial elites as well. Other identities were formed in opposition to the empires, especially during the Qing. The imaginary of Koreans as better Confucians and guardians of righteousness than the Chinese or their rulers belong among these. I have accepted that "nationalism" is a possible term for this compound singularity, as long as we recognize that it was nationalism of a peculiar kind, in which the limitation of claims was sometimes as significant as their extension, and in which there was a lot of acknowledged cultural borrowing and hybridity.

But even if we do accept that Korean concepts of nation existed during the Chosŏn era, twentieth-century forms of nationalism took over the identifications of the past, systematized them, and made them much more cohesive and exclusionary. This new kind of nationalism, inspired by European models, attempted to displace all other identities with a narrow definition of the nation. In Korea, as we have seen, the process was intensified by the counterpressure of Japanese colonization. In China, where nationalists faced the almost impossible task of remaking an empire as a nation, Communism in the end furnished a solution of sorts: By claiming that the Chinese Communist Party was acting on behalf of all people who lived within the borders of the Qing empire, it managed to produce, at least in theory, a Chinese nation (*Zhonghua minzu*) that consisted of fifty-five "nationalities" plus the Chinese, the 96 percent of the population now redefined as the "Han nationality."[4] The concept presupposes that everyone who lives within the current borders of the PRC and Taiwan—the Chinese homeland (*guojia*)—belongs to the Chinese nation, and has, in principle, done so for a very long time.

In spite of significant differences in both their genesis and their substance, these nationalisms leave limited space for the hybridity of past forms of sovereignty. On the contrary, they imagine fully independent, unitary statehood for the "nation" as the only possible outcome of nationalist ideas and practices. Their concept of relations between China and Korea is similar to inter-state relations among any states in the international state system. For Korean nationalists, irrespective of their origins and overall orientation, China is another country—a big, close-by, and therefore important country, but still another country, in all respects delimited from Korea. In this matter there are few differences between perceptions in the North and the South, and North Korean nationalism toward all other countries is, if anything, even stronger than that in the South.

But nationalisms in their modern form—powerful as they are in both China and Korea—cannot fully negate history, culture, and geography. There is little doubt that today's Chinese

Communist leaders believe that their country has a special relationship with Korea that is circumscribed by the past and by
adjacency. This sense of connection exceeds China's links with
any other country along its extensive borders. For the Communists, the Korean War, which was fought on their watch, looms
particularly large in this image. But the countless hours I have
spent discussing Korea with officials in Beijing have convinced
me that the paternalistic view of a unique Chinese responsibility
for Korea is alive and well in the Chinese capital. As representatives of a party that throughout its existence has been willing
to sacrifice the lives of large numbers of their own countrymen
in the name of its great causes, among which nationalism has
been a very significant one, the fact that the North Korean regime is responsible for untold human tragedies does not rank
very high in CCP perceptions. What is more important is that
the north has been willing to pay at least lip service to the
principle of China's centrality within the region and is free of
(other) foreign influence. As one former top official explained
to me, the DPRK is the real Korea, because it does not have
US influence in it. The South is contaminated through American control and is therefore not a genuine Korean state.

As we have seen in this book, adjacency also matters greatly,
both in China and in Korea. On the Chinese side, the fear that
Korea could be unified in alliance with outsiders remains a strategic concern, as it was in the sixteenth and in the twentieth
century. The old saying about "lips and teeth" still crops up often
when discussing China and Korea: When the lips are gone, the
teeth get cold. This is in essence an argument for Korea (or, now,
half of Korea) as a Chinese buffer state, and is of course very

hard for any Korean nationalist to accept. Even so, it is often used in Seoul to signify just how significant Korea is for China, among both those who argue that the road to Korean unification goes through Beijing and those who are fearful that any weakening of the US-ROK security alliance will lead to Chinese predominance over all of the Korean Peninsula.

Today it is hard to judge what significance ideology has in the China–Korea relationship, beyond the view of the North as being untainted by Western imperialism. It is clear that very few Chinese leaders feel much personal affinity with the DPRK, even if both claim to be socialist states led by Communist parties. North Korean and Chinese societies are vastly different; China is richer and freer than anything ordinary North Koreans can even dream of. In private, Chinese officials shake their heads over North Korean backwardness and obstinacy, a bit like Qing officials did back in the nineteenth century. But there is also an element of sympathy, even admiration, for the way Pyongyang stands up to the United States and Japan. Views of how China should handle the DPRK are very varied among today's officials in Beijing, but there are few who do not believe that the joint sacrifices in the Korean War and the fact that North Korea is a "People's Republic," like China, would make it harder for even the most Realpolitik-minded of Chinese leaders to fully wash their hands of the DPRK. Meanwhile, there are those on the Chinese Communist side who would claim that South Korea's lively democracy and open society is a threat to the PRC, especially if it were to extend all the way to China's borders.

On the South Korean side, as we have seen, views have been changing faster, and not to China's advantage. Given the explosion in economic interaction between the two countries and the profound skepticism that predominates at least among liberal and left-wing South Koreans toward the United States, one would have expected that many today would prioritize relations with China. Instead, the opposite has happened, at least in terms of public opinion. China's silence on North Korean attacks against South Koreans, its ham-fisted attempts to punish Korean businesses over the THAAD affair, and the general lack of warmth with which it has greeted the new liberal South Korean government, has convinced an increasing number of South Korean leaders that China will not be a trustworthy partner in regional affairs, whatever happens in the future. Instead many South Koreans have begun to believe that China is the main impediment against national unification, and some suspect that Beijing's long-term aim is to de facto annex North Korea as a part of a greater Chinese zone of control.

The fact that the immense rise in China's economic power does not easily translate into diplomatic or political power, at least not on such a thorny issue as Korea, has surprised many younger Chinese leaders. Their nationalism expects, and their policies are built on, a gradual accommodation of all countries in the eastern Asian region to the centrality of China's position. This is the premise for the Belt and Road initiatives, for the Asian Infrastructure Investment Bank, and for the Shanghai Cooperation Organization. They assume that the United States and Japan will attempt to delay the forward march of China's regional position, but they do not expect such policies to be successful. The view in Beijing is that, over time at least, the rest of the region will need China's cooperation more than they need that of the Americans. Korea, and especially the North Korean nuclear crises, serve as unwelcome reminders for Beijing that all is not well with their country's presumed irresistible rise to regional predomination.

Views in Beijing on Korean affairs are therefore probably more diverse today than they have been at any point since the founding of the People's Republic. The majority view, at least at the moment, is that stability is best for China. The ideal would be a return to the Six-Party Talks under Chinese auspices, ending either in full North Korean denuclearization (which is regarded as extremely unlikely) or an agreement to strictly limit North Korean nuclear and missile capabilities through international inspections. Spurred by a relaxation of tension, North Korea would undertake at least limited internal economic reform, making a domestic breakdown less likely. To further this stability scenario, China's current leaders would probably also support bilateral agreements between the DPRK and the United States that would lead in the same direction, even if they happened outside the Six-Party framework. What China will not do is offer to act as an intermediary or a guarantor, unless it happens in a multilateral setting, or put so much pressure on the DPRK that the regime collapses. Chinese president Xi Jinping believes that China has too much to lose from being responsible for international arrangements that may not hold or from any dramatic change in the North Korean polity.

The problem with this majority view is that, given Korea's history, it is built on exceedingly optimistic premises. At the moment North Korea refuses to return to the Six-Party Talks or to strike a bilateral deal with the United States. It is quite likely that some form of nuclear and missile testing will be restarted by the North Koreans, leading to further crises. Meanwhile, there are few signs that the North Korean state will undertake significant economic reform, out of fear that the Kim family regime under such circumstances may lose too much control over society. At the moment North Korea is not able to feed itself, and in May 2019 the UN reported that about 40 percent of the North's population was in urgent need of food aid.[5] On the US side, it is almost impossible to imagine any administration settling for less than a promise of full North Korean nuclear disarmament. In the South, President Moon's term will end in early 2022, and he cannot stand for reelection. He may well be replaced by a president less inclined to make concessions to the North. Long-term stability under present conditions therefore seems very unlikely.

It is therefore distinctly possible that the situation on the Korean Peninsula will stumble from crisis to crisis, with China unwilling to take on more of a role than what it has at present (meaning, providing the aid that the DPRK needs to survive, while encouraging its leaders toward domestic reform and foreign constraint). Some Chinese critics of current policy on Korea argue not only that this approach has failed to bring meaningful results so far, but also that in the future it runs the triple risk of highlighting North Korean impropriety, South Korean anguish, and Chinese passivity. Such an outcome, critics argue, may lead to unwanted spillover, in China's relations both with the United States and, crucially, with its eastern Asian neighbors in the south and west. A Chinese acquaintance in the foreign policy establishment, who also happens to be a relative hard-liner on

Sino-American affairs, argues that China needs to force Pyong-yang to pay more attention to China's interests. "If you are a rising great power, and you have a next door neighbor, allied with you, who treats you very badly, why should others treat you with respect?" he argues. In other words, why should the Philippines, for instance, be exceedingly heedful of China's interests, when the North Koreans get away with treating the great power next door very shoddily?

Such questions are undoubtedly similar to questions asked at the Ming and Qing courts in the past. Then there were always limits to what a Korean state could get away with vis-à-vis China without facing serious displeasure and possibly the threat of intervention. Still, on the whole, such matters were usually settled through the empire making clear its demands and the Koreans complying, at least verbally. The only occasions when the empire did intervene, was when confronted with peer rivals on the Korean Peninsula, as with Hideyoshi in the sixteenth century, the Ming-Qing rivalry in the seventeenth, Meiji Japan in the nineteenth, and the Americans in the twentieth. Maybe there is a lesson here as well. The US presence in South Korea reduces China's ability to influence the North, but it may lead China to intervene militarily if it sees events in Korea as turning against it. The most likely such scenario is the sudden and unexpected breakdown of the North Korean regime, possibly through outside actions against it, but more likely as an outcome of its domestic dysfunctions.

What would China do in the case of such a breakdown? I have little doubt that it would intervene in some form, if only to take control of a buffer zone at the border. Chinese authorities are dead set on preventing an unprecedented influx of foreign refugees across its frontiers. What more it would do depends on the circumstances. It may act to secure the DPRK's weapons of mass destruction, alone or working with the United States, which is the power that is by far best capable of such operations. And it would probably assist with relief aid for the North Korean population. First and foremost China would attempt to position itself to have a decisive influence on how Korea is reunified, with guarantees of neutrality and denuclearization. It is also likely that it will ask for trade concessions from South Korea as part of the price for being cooperative in negotiations of reunification.

The core dilemma for China's long-term Korea policy is this: Most Beijing experts believe deep down that a united, prosperous Korea would be better for China in the long run than the current situation. And the majority of Chinese Korea specialists seem to think that North Korea, in its present form, cannot survive long-term without domestic reform of the kind that Kim Jong-un has so far refused to carry out. Some hope that de-escalation of tension on the peninsula will provide the incentive for market reforms in the North, on which China could have a major influence, and also provide hope for economic integration between the two Korean states. Most think that that cannot happen under the Kim regime. But the current Chinese leadership, having made stability their mantra for Korea, seems fearful of any change in Pyongyang, lest it be to Beijing's disadvantage. This dilemma has made some East Asians wonder whether any fundamental change is possible in Korea until there are changes in the Chinese government.

There is little doubt that North Korea has turned into an abhorrent regime that is responsible for massive crimes against its own population. Its demise, at least if it happened suddenly, could, however, turn into East Asia's moment of truth, the way Hideyoshi's invasions did in the sixteenth century. Is China ready to put the interests of the larger region above its own? Can an authoritarian China accept, and even facilitate, the unification of Korea under a democratic government? Will East Asia's long peace, its generation of avoiding war, hold when power in Korea is again up for grabs? History may be a guide to how we understand these problems, but it will not give us definite answers. Only current and future policymakers can do that.

Meanwhile, in the wider context, many will be watching Beijing's Korean policy for signs of how China will behave when it *has* risen internationally. Like in the early Ming and Qing empires, China's Korean policies can easily be seen as a weathervane of how China will behave toward others, farther afield. So far, the evidence is only in a limited way encouraging. The PRC's willingness to work with others to help solve the North Korean nuclear crisis is a good sign, but its high-handed approach toward South Korea and its inability or indisposition to induce any kind of change in North Korean behavior are not. In the minds of others, such attitudes produce unfavorable images of China's authoritarianism and its past as a hegemonic empire. So far, China's Korean policy has led it to the worst of all worlds as far as foreign perceptions go: A rising great power that is fearful of playing a transformational international role, even at its own borders, while protecting an abominable regime and opposing a popular and democratic one. It is not the best starting point for China as a future world power.

When one walks around in Seoul, with its LED-lit shopping arcades, cosmetics stores, and high-end restaurants, listening to young people talk about their favorite music or YouTube stars, it is hard to believe that North Korea is only thirty-five miles away, about as far as the full length of New York's Broadway. This very different world could literally be up the street. It is also hard to believe that young Chinese, who, irrespective of geography and politics, live in a cultural world so infinitely much closer to that of Seoul than to that of Pyongyang, will end up protecting and preserving the North Korean nightmare for simple reasons of *realpolitik*. But that is where we are today, and neither is it uncommon in history, including that of US foreign policy. If history is a guide, the best that we can hope for at this moment in Korea is, first, arms control, then détente between North and South, and finally a Chinese policy of letting North Korea go when the regime starts to unravel. The worst that we can fear is war. In a globalized world, the relationship between China and Korea, so long in the making, so intense in its composition, has the potential of influencing how all of us live our lives, one way or the other.

NOTES

1. China and the Chosŏn State

1. I use the term "country" here in a very general sense. Both China and Korea could as easily be seen primarily as cultures (and intermingled cultures at that), at least up to the Ming / Chosŏn era.

2. For Koryŏ forms of identity, see Remco E. Breuker, *Establishing a Pluralist Society in Medieval Korea, 918–1170: History, Ideology, and Identity in the Koryŏ Dynasty* (Leiden: Brill, 2010). For a fundamental anthropological discussion of concepts of identity, see Fredrik Barth, introduction to *Ethnic Groups and Boundaries: The Social Organization of Culture Difference,* ed. Fredrik Barth (Boston: Little, Brown, 1969).

3. In order to help with identification, in this book I use pinyin (for Chinese [without diacritics]) and McCune-Reischauer (for Korean) transliterations as much as possible. The exceptions are place names and personal names that are well known in English in a different form, or when individuals prefer another spelling of their names.

4. There were early forms of alphabetic or mixed-use scripts in Korea at least from the second century CE, but none of these were used widely or long-term, even for nonofficial purposes.

5. Nanyue is a particularly instructive counterexample to Korea, given that almost all of this border-state's territory was incorporated into the empire during Han times. See Erica Brindley, *Ancient China and the Yue: Perceptions and Identities on the Southern Frontier, c. 400 BCE–50 CE* (Cambridge: Cambridge University Press, 2015); and Brindley, "Representations

and Uses of Yue Identity along the Southern Frontier of the Han, Ca. 200–111 BCE," *Early China* 33 / 34 (2010): 1–35.

6. One good definition of empire is Burbank and Cooper's: "Empires are large political units, expansionist or with a memory of power extended over space, polities that maintain distinction and hierarchy as they incorporate new people." Jane Burbank and Frederick Cooper, *Empires in World History: Power and the Politics of Difference* (Princeton, NJ: Princeton University Press, 2010), 3.

7. There is significant debate among historians about whether it is meaningful to use the Western term "empire" for non-Western state formations, such as those in eastern Asia. It seems to me to be a useful term for what East Asians, at least since the Song era, have called a "great state" (*daguo* in Chinese, or *daeguk* in Korean); see Timothy Brook, "Great States," *Journal of Asian Studies* 75, no. 4 (November 2016): 957–972. Strikingly, the only modern Asian state that has kept the concept in its name is *Daehan minguk* (the Republic of [Great] Korea), present-day South Korea.

8. See Jennifer E. Sessions, *By Sword and Plow: France and the Conquest of Algeria* (Ithaca, NY: Cornell University Press, 2011); and John Patrick Montano, *The Roots of English Colonialism in Ireland* (Cambridge: Cambridge University Press, 2011).

9. See Walter Scheidel, ed., *Rome and China: Comparative Perspectives on Ancient World Empires* (Oxford: Oxford University Press, 2009); Scheidel, ed., *State Power in Ancient China and Rome* (Oxford: Oxford University Press, 2015); and Fritz-Heiner Mutschler and Achim Mittag, eds., *Conceiving the Empire: China and Rome Compared* (Oxford: Oxford University Press, 2008). For a comparative view of European empires, see Krishan Kumar, *Visions of Empire: How Five Imperial Regimes Shaped the World* (Princeton, NJ: Princeton University Press, 2017); and for comparisons in Asia, see Brian P. Farrell and Jack Fairey, eds., *Empire in Asia: A New Global History*, vol. 1 (London: Bloomsbury, 2018).

10. The literature on comparative Chinese empires is remarkably weak. For attempts at rectifying this, see Hilde De Weerdt, Chu Ming-Kin, and Ho Hou-Ieong, "Chinese Empires in Comparative Perspective: A Digital Approach," *Verge: Studies in Global Asias* 2, no. 2 (2016): 58–69. For a broader comparison, see Peter F. Bang and C. A. Bayly, eds., *Tributary Empires in Global History* (London: Palgrave Macmillan, 2011).

11. For Qing expansionism, see Peter C. Perdue, "Comparing Empires: Manchu Colonialism," *International History Review* 20, no. 2 (June 1, 1998): 255–262.

12. See Zsombor Rajkai and Ildikó Bellér-Hann, eds., *Frontiers and Boundaries: Encounters on China's Margins* (Wiesbaden: Harrassowitz, 2012); Kathlene Baldanza, *Ming China and Vietnam: Negotiating Borders in Early Modern Asia* (Cambridge: Cambridge University Press, 2016); Diana Lary, ed., *The Chinese State at the Borders* (Vancouver: UBC Press, 2007), especially the chapters by Alexander Woodside and Timothy Brook; Peter C. Perdue, "Crossing Borders in Imperial China," in *Asia Inside Out: Connected Places,* ed. Eric Tagliacozzo, Helen F. Siu, and Peter C. Perdue (Cambridge, MA: Harvard University Press, 2015), 195–218. For the Han origins, see Nicola Di Cosmo, "Han Frontiers: Toward an Integrated View," *Journal of the American Oriental Society* 129, no. 2 (April 2009): 199–214.

13. See Mei-yu Hsieh and Mark Edward Lewis, "Tianxia and the Invention of Empire in East Asia," in *Chinese Visions of World Order: Tianxia, Culture, and World Politics,* ed. Ban Wang (Durham, NC: Duke University Press, 2017), 25–48; Wang Mingming, "All under Heaven (Tianxia): Cosmological Perspectives and Political Ontologies in Pre-Modern China," *HAU: Journal of Ethnographic Theory* 2, no. 1 (March 1, 2012): 337–383; Zhao Tingyang, *Tianxia tixi: Shijie zhidu zhexue daolun* [The Tianxia system: An introduction to an institution in global thinking] (Nanjing: Jiangsu jiaoyu, 2005).

14. See J. K. Fairbank and S. Y. Teng, "On the Ch'ing Tributary System," *Harvard Journal of Asiatic Studies* 6, no. 2 (1941): 135–246; and, for a recent critique, Peter C. Perdue, "The Tenacious Tributary System," *Journal of Contemporary China* 24, no. 96 (November 2, 2015): 1002–1014.

15. See Pamela Kyle Crossley, Helen F. Siu, and Donald S. Sutton, eds., *Empire at the Margins: Culture, Ethnicity, and Frontier in Early Modern China* (Berkeley: University of California Press, 2006); and Feng Zhang, *Chinese Hegemony: Grand Strategy and International Institutions in East Asian History* (Stanford, CA: Stanford University Press, 2015), esp. chaps. 2 and 3. See also Brook, "Great States," for a terminological discussion of empire and vassals.

16. The best comparative discussion, including of concepts of sovereignty (which we will return to in the Conclusion), is in Timothy Brook, M. C. van Walt van Praag, and Miek Boltjes, *Sacred Mandates: Asian International Relations since Chinggis Khan* (Chicago: University of Chicago Press, 2018).

17. Timothy Brook, *The Troubled Empire: China in the Yuan and Ming Dynasties* (Cambridge, MA: Harvard University Press, 2010).

18. The now-classic study is Frederic E. Wakeman, *The Great Enterprise: The Manchu Reconstruction of Imperial Order in Seventeenth-Century China*, 2 vols. (Berkeley: University of California Press, 1985).

19. John Gallagher and Ronald Robinson, "The Imperialism of Free Trade," *Economic History Review* 6, no. 1 (1953): 1–15; for the original use of the term, see C. R. Fay, "Chapter XI: The Movement towards Free Trade, 1820–1853," in *The Cambridge History of the British Empire*, vol. 2 (Cambridge: Cambridge University Press, 1940).

20. Wang Gungwu has pointed out, "There could not surely be a stable [tribute] system without power, sustained power." Wang Gungwu, "Early Ming Relations with Southeast Asia," in *The Chinese World Order*, ed. John King Fairbank (Cambridge, MA; Harvard University Press, 1968), 60.

21. It is also the topic of Kirk W. Larsen, *Tradition, Treaties, and Trade: Qing Imperialism and Korea, 1850–1910* (Cambridge, MA: Harvard University Asia Center, 2011). As will be obvious from Chapter 2, I have learned a great deal from Professor Larsen, and I am extremely grateful to him for coming to Cambridge to comment on the Reischauer Lectures on which this book is based.

22. JaHyun Kim Haboush, *The Great East Asian War and the Birth of the Korean Nation* (New York: Columbia University Press, 2016), 13.

23. Ki-mun Yi and Robert Ramsey, *A History of the Korean Language* (Cambridge: Cambridge University Press, 2011).

24. This is pretty close to the current *Oxford English Dictionary* definition.

25. Diderot's *Encyclopédie*, published in 1765, defines a nation as "a considerable number of people, who live in a specific area of land, within specific boundaries, and obey the same government" (Denis Diderot and Jean le Rond d'Alembert, eds., *Encyclopédie, ou dictionnaire raisonné des*

sciences, des arts et des métiers, etc. (Paris, 1765), 11:36, s.v. "Nation"). Jacob Grimm's 1846 definition of a people, which became built into so many European national projects, is very different: "A people is the essence of all those who speak the same language"; quoted in Jürgen Habermas, *The Postnational Constellation: Political Essays* (London: Polity Press, 2001), 6. By the 1840s, territory and polity had been replaced by culture as the common denominator.

26. Mazzini, *Doveri del'uomo* [Duties of man], 3rd ed. (Rome, 1873), 21.

27. Ernest Renan, "What Is a Nation?," in *Becoming National: A Reader*, ed. Geoff Eley and Ronald Grigor Suny (Oxford: Oxford University Press, 1996), 52.

28. Krishan Kumar, "Nation-States as Empires, Empires as Nation-States: Two Principles, One Practice?," *Theory and Society* 39, no. 2 (2010): 119–143, 133.

29. Eugen Weber, *Peasants into Frenchmen: The Modernization of Rural France, 1870–1914* (Stanford, CA: Stanford University Press, 1976), 485.

30. Charles Maier, *Among Empires: American Ascendancy and Its Predecessors* (Cambridge, MA: Harvard University Press, 2006), 28–29.

31. If proof is needed, a study of Yugoslav and post-Yugoslav history is recommended.

32. And for early modern Korea, there were, of course, also questions about who to exclude: Were slaves fully part of the *guk?* Or Cheju islanders? I am grateful to Carter Eckert for this point.

33. There is inspiration in Prasenjit Duara, *Rescuing History from the Nation: Questioning Narratives of Modern China* (Chicago: University of Chicago Press, 1995). For Korea, see Stella Xu, *Reconstructing Ancient Korean History: The Formation of Korean-ness in the Shadow of History* (Lanham, MD: Lexington Books, 2016).

34. Chung-Ying Cheng, "On Yi as a Universal Principle of Specific Application in Confucian Morality," *Philosophy East and West* 22, no. 3 (1972): 269–280.

35. This term, which keeps appearing in Korean history, has come to mean "a volunteer army" or even "a people's force."

36. In Chinese known as lixue 理學 (The Principles' School) of Confucian thinking.

37. Peter Bol, *Neo-Confucianism in History* (Cambridge, MA: Harvard University Press, 2008), is a fine overview.

38. For an overview of Zhu Xi's thinking, see Wing-tsit Chan, ed., *Chu Hsi and Neo-Confucianism* (Honolulu: University of Hawai'i Press, 1986).

39. See Daniel Gardner, *Zhu Xi's Reading of the Analects: Canon, Commentary, and the Classical Tradition* (New York: Columbia University Press, 2003). See also Tsong-han Lee, "Different Mirrors of the Past: Southern Song Historiography" (PhD diss., Harvard University, 2008); and Lee, "Making Moral Decisions: Zhu Xi's 'Outline and Details of the Comprehensive Mirror for Aid in Government,'" *Journal of Song-Yuan Studies* 39, no. 1 (2009).

40. Chung-ying Ch'eng, *New Dimensions of Confucian and Neo-Confucian Philosophy: Contemporary Allegory and the Search for Postmodern Faith* (Albany: SUNY Press, 1991), 235.

41. To the point of holding up officials who refused to serve the new regime out of loyalty to the old as examples of what the Chosŏn expected of its own officials.

42. See Edward Y. J. Chung, *The Korean Neo-Confucianism of Yi T'oegye and Yi Yulgok: A Reappraisal of the "Four-Seven Thesis" and Its Practical Implications for Self-Cultivation* (Albany: SUNY Press, 1995); Hwang Yi, *A Korean Confucian Way of Life and Thought: The Chasongnok (Record of Self-Reflection) by Yi Hwang (Toegye)*, trans. Edward Y. J. Chung (Honolulu: University of Hawai'i Press, 2016); Young-chan Ro, *The Korean Neo-Confucianism of Yi Yulgok* (Albany: SUNY Press, 1989); Lee Jung-Chul, "Yi I kyŏngseron ŭi sŏngnipkwa kŭ chŏngch'ijŏk paegyŏng" [Yi Yulgok's statecraft theory and its political setting], *Sa Ch'ong* 75 (2012).

43. Byonghyon Choi, trans., *The Annals of King T'aejo: Founder of Korea's Chosŏn Dynasty* (Cambridge, MA: Harvard University Press, 2014), 142.

44. On the Korean side, see Michael Charles Kalton, "The Neo-Confucian World View and Value System of Yi Dynasty Korea" (PhD diss., Harvard University, 1977).

45. For a good introduction to the early Ming, see Brook, *The Troubled Empire*.

46. The best recent treatment of Ming foreign relations is Zhang, *Chinese Hegemony;* see also Wan Ming, *Mingdai Zhong-wai guanxi shi*

Iungao [A history of Chinese foreign relations during the Ming Empire] (Beijing: Zhongguo shehui kexue, 2011).

47. Huang Zhangjian, ed., *Ming shi lu* [Annals of the Ming empire] (Nan'gang: Zhongyang yanjiuyuan lishi yuyan yanjiusuo, 1966), bk. 44, 866–867. Author's translation, building on parts of the translated text in Zhang, *Chinese Hegemony*.

48. Quoted from Zhang, *Chinese Hegemony*, 60. See also Dane Alston, "Emperor and Emissary: The Hongwu Emperor, Kwŏn Kŭn, and the Poetry of Late Fourteenth Century Diplomacy," *Korean Studies* 32, no. 1 (2008): 104–147.

49. For early Chosŏn, see John B. Duncan, *The Origins of the Chosŏn Dynasty* (Seattle: University of Washington Press, 2000).

50. Quoted in Haesung Lee, "The Neo-Confucianism of the Joseon Dynasty: Its Theoretical Foundation and Main Issues," *Asian Studies* 4, no. 1 (February 29, 2016): 187.

51. Lee, "The Neo-Confucianism."

52. The best overview is still Martina Deuchler, *The Confucian Transformation of Korea: A Study of Society and Ideology* (Cambridge, MA: Harvard University Press, 1992).

53. *Ming shi lu*, bk. 228, 3324–3325.

54. Liang Hui Wang II, in *Mengzi* (Beijing: Zhonghua shuju, 1998).

55. See Deuchler, *Confucian Transformation of Korea*.

56. Quoted in Zhang, *Chinese Hegemony*, 76.

57. Authority-wise, things did not become better for the Ming when the then-former Zhengtong emperor suddenly reappeared from his Mongol incarceration, never mind when he reclaimed the throne in 1457 (with the somewhat ironic reign name Tianshun—"obedience to Heaven"). Even so, Tianshun informed Lê Thánh Tông, the ruler of Dai Viet, "We are the Emperor, and having received Heaven's great mandate, We rule the *hua* and the *yi*. One culture provides the norm for all places, its influence transforming all beyond the four quarters. Of all who are vaulted by Heaven and sustained by Earth, there is none who does not submit in heart" (quoted in Brook, Walt van Praag, and Boltjes, *Sacred Mandates*, 65).

58. Joshua J. Van Lieu, "Chosŏn-Qing Tributary Discourse: Transgression, Restoration, and Textual Performativity," *Cross-Currents: East Asian History and Culture Review*, no. 27 (2018): 81.

59. Lieu, 86.

60. See Donald N. Clark, "Sino-Korean Tributary Relations under the Ming," in *The Cambridge History of China*, vol. 8: *The Ming Dynasty*, ed. Denis C. Twitchett and Frederick W. Mote (Cambridge: Cambridge University Press, 1998), 272–300.

61. The example is from Seung B. Kye, "Huddling under the Imperial Umbrella: A Korean Approach to Ming China in the Early 1500s," *Journal of Korean Studies* 15, no. 1 (2010): 41–66.

62. Gakusho Nakajima, "The Structure and Transformation of the Ming Tribute Trade System," in *Global History and New Polycentric Approaches: Europe, Asia and the Americas in a World Network System*, ed. Manuel Perez Garcia and Lucio De Sousa (Singapore: Springer Singapore, 2018), 137–162.

63. Sunglim Kim, *Flowering Plums and Curio Cabinets: The Culture of Objects in Late Chosŏn Korean Art* (Seattle: University of Washington Press, 2018), 73

64. Qian Chengjun, "A Research Review of Chinese Books Exchanged between Ancient China, Japan and Korea and Their Influence," in *The History and Cultural Heritage of Chinese Calligraphy, Printing and Library Work*, ed. Susan M. Allen, Lin Zuzao, Cheng Xiaolan, and Jan Bos (Berlin: de Gruyter, 2010).

65. Ku Do-young, "16segi Chosŏn taemyŏng sahaengdanŭi chŏngbosujipkwa chŏngboryŏk (The Intelligence-Gathering Strength of the Chosŏn Envoys to Ming in the 16th Century)," *Taedong munhwa yŏn'gu* 95 (2016): 85–120.

66. Quoted in Ji-Young Lee, *China's Hegemony: Four Hundred Years of East Asian Domination* (New York: Columbia University Press, 2016), 107, 108.

67. Quoted from William Theodore De Bary, Donald Keene, George Tanabe, and Paul Varley, eds., *Sources of Japanese Tradition*, vol. 1 (New York: Columbia University Press, 2001), 467.

68. For overviews of the wars that followed, in addition to Haboush, see Han Myŏng-gi, *Imjin Waeran kwa Han-Chung kwan'gye* [Korea-China relations during the Imjin War] (Seoul: Yŏksa Pip'yŏngsa, 1999); and Ji-Young Lee, *The Imjin War (1592–1598)* (New York: Columbia University Press, 2016).

69. Quoted in Yoshi Saburo Kuno, *Japanese Expansion on the Asiatic Continent: A Study in the History of Japan with Special Reference to Her International Relations with China, Korea, and Russia* (Berkeley: University of California Press, 1937), 304. I have kept the original translation's term "nation," although "country" may be more appropriate here.

70. Haboush, *Great East Asian War,* 80. See also J. Marshall Craig, "Visions of China, Korea, and Japan in the East Asian War, 1592–1598" (DPhil thesis, Oxford University, 2015).

71. Harriet T. Zurndorfer, "Wanli China versus Hideyoshi's Japan: Rethinking China's Involvement in the Imjin Waeran," in *The East Asian War, 1592–1598: International Relations, Violence, and Memory,* ed. James Bryant Lewis (Abingdon, UK: Routledge, 2015), 197–235; James B. Lewis, "The Wanli Emperor and Ming China's Defence of Korea against Japan," *International Journal of Asian Studies* 8, no. 1 (January 2011): 73–80.

72. Haboush, *Great East Asian War,* 94–95.

73. Quoted from Han Myŏng-gi, *Imjin Waeran,* 32.

74. Haboush, *Great East Asian War,* 34.

75. Zurndorfer, "Wanli China," 213.

76. Quoted from Robert Kong Chan, *Korea-China Relations in History and Contemporary Implications* (London: Palgrave Macmillan, 2017), 96.

77. Chan, 97–108.

78. For an overview of early Chosŏn-Qing relations, see Lim Jongtae, "Tributary Relations between the Chosŏn and Ch'ing Courts to 1800," *The Cambridge History of China,* vol. 9: *The Ch'ing Dynasty to 1800, Part Two,* ed. Willard J. Peterson (Cambridge: Cambridge University Press, 2016), 146–196.

79. This is a key point with regard to the so-called New Qing History, which emphasizes the multiethnic origins and practices of the Qing, as well as the self-identification of the imperial clan as being separate from but equally superior to all the various ethnicities and religions that the empire consisted of. For its origins, see Evelyn S. Rawski, "Reenvisioning the Qing: The Significance of the Qing Period in Chinese History," *Journal of Asian Studies* 55, no. 4 (1996): 829–850; Joanna Waley-Cohen, "The New Qing History," *Radical History Review* 88, no. 1 (January 2004): 193–206. See also Ding Yizhuang and Mark Elliott, "How to Write

Chinese History in the Twenty-First Century: The Impact of the 'New Qing History' Studies and Chinese Responses," *Chinese Studies in History* 51, no. 1 (January 2018): 70–95.

80. In a few cases, Korean scholars of the late seventeenth century began using the term *Zhonghua* (Central Florescence, an ancient name for China and its culture) for Chosŏn; see Chŏng Ok-cha, *Chŏson hugi Chŏson Chunghwa sasang yŏn'gu* [A study of the idea of a Chŏson Zhonghua in late Chŏson] (Seoul: Ilchisa, 1998). For some Chŏson scholars, at least, neo-Confucian learning may also have been gradually universalized in the sense that its rootedness in China may have become less significant, not unlike how we today would apply quantum mechanics without thinking about its German origins (I am grateful to Carter Eckert for this suggestion).

81. See Joshua J. Van Lieu, "Divergent Visions of Serving the Great: The Emergence of Chosŏn-Qing Tributary Relations as a Politics of Representation" (PhD diss., University of Washington, 2010). See also, on Chinese Ming loyalists in Korea, Adam Bohnet, "Ruling Ideology and Marginal Subjects: Ming Loyalism and Foreign Lineages in Late Chosŏn Korea," *Journal of Early Modern History* 15, no. 6 (January 2011): 477–505.

82. This is not to deny that Koreans were active participants in the international trade patterns that expanded in the seventeenth and eighteenth centuries, only that the cultural effects of such contacts were less visible at home, mainly due to government policies; see Seonmin Kim, *Ginseng and Borderland: Territorial Boundaries and Political Relations between Qing China and Choson Korea, 1636–1912* (Berkeley: University of California Press, 2017).

83. For the contrast with Vietnam, see Liam Kelley, "Convergence and Conflict: Dai Viet in the Sinic Order," in Brook, Walt van Praag, and Boltjes, *Sacred Mandates;* and Jaymin Kim, "The Rule of Ritual: Crimes and Justice in Qing-Vietnamese Relations during the Qianlong Period (1736–1796)," in *China's Encounters on the South and Southwest: Reforging the Fiery Frontier over Two Millennia,* ed. James A. Anderson and John K. Whitmore (Leiden: Brill, 2014).

84. For an overview, see Gari Ledyard, "Korean Travelers in China over Four Hundred Years, 1488–1887," *Occasional Papers on Korea,* no. 2 (1974): 1–42.

85. See Kwon Nae-Hyun, "Chosŏn Korea's Trade with Qing China and the Circulation of Silver," *Acta Koreana* 18, no. 1 (June 2015): 163–185; and Zhang Cunwu, *Qing-Han zongfan maoyi, 1637–1894* [Sino-Korean tributary trade, 1637–1894] (Taibei: Zhongyang yanjiuyuan jindaishi yanjiusuo, 1985).

86. Shin Ik-Cheol, "Perceptions of the West in Chŏson Travel Accounts: Chŏson Encounters with the 'West' in Beijing," SOAS-AKS Working Papers in Korean Studies (London: SOAS, 2009), 12. The first Korean Christians were probably baptized in Beijing in the 1780s.

87. Cheol, 10–11.

88. Bonnie Kim, "'Closed' Encounters: The Arrival of the West in Nineteenth-Century Korea" (PhD diss., Columbia University, 2006), 67.

89. Kim, 125; statements by Korean Christian under investigation.

2. THE INTERNATIONALIZATION OF EAST ASIA

1. Quoted in Paul Beirne, "The Eclectic Mysticism of Ch'oe Cheu," *Review of Korean Studies* 2 (1999): 160. See also Beirne, *Su-Un and His World of Symbols: The Founder of Korea's First Indigenous Religion* (London: Routledge, 2016), 160.

2. Chang Po-un, "Ap'yŏnjŏnjaengŭl parabonŭn chosŏnŭi tajung shisŏn: 19segi chunghuban chosŏn chojŏng, chishikch'ŭng, sŏminch'ŭngŭi taech'ŏnginshik yŏn'gu" [Multiple views of the Opium Wars in the Chosŏn dynasty: A study on the Chosŏn government's, intellectuals', and commoners' perceptions of the Qing Dynasty in the mid- to late-19th century], *Han'guk sasang sahak* 56 (2017): 132.

3. Zhang Baoyun [Chang Po-un], "Joseon Dynasty's Perceptions of the Qing Dynasty in the 1860s and 1870s," *Journal of Koreanology* 61 (November 2016): 158.

4. Yi Hang-no, "Sinify the Western Barbarians," in *Sourcebook of Korean Civilization*, vol. 2, ed. Peter H. Lee (New York: Columbia University Press, 1992), 158–159.

5. The best overview is still Martina Deuchler, *Confucian Gentlemen and Barbarian Envoys: The Opening of Korea, 1875–1885* (Seattle: University of Washington Press, 1977). See also Jean-Francois Gossiaux, "Pourquoi changer d'ancêtres? Le colonialisme français en échec (Corée, 1866)"

[Why change ancestors? A setback for French colonialism (Korea, 1866)], *L'Homme*, no. 202 (2012): 141–168.

6. See Gordon H. Chang, "Whose 'Barbarism'? Whose 'Treachery'? Race and Civilization in the Unknown United States–Korea War of 1871," *Journal of American History* 89, no. 4 (March 2003), 1331–1365.

7. For an overview of this era, see Key-Hiuk Kim, *The Last Phase of the East Asian World Order: Korea, Japan, and the Chinese Empire, 1860–1882* (Berkeley: University of California Press, 1980).

8. Yŏng-ho Ch'oe, "The *Kapsin* Coup of 1884: A Reassessment," *Korean Studies* 6, no. 1 (1982): 105–124.

9. On these forms of thinking, see Kirk W. Larsen, *Tradition, Treaties, and Trade: Qing Imperialism and Korea, 1850–1910* (Cambridge, MA: Harvard University Asia Center, 2011).

10. See Carter Eckert, "Conclusion," in *Colonial Modernity in Korea,* ed. Shin Gi-Wook and Michael E. Robinson (Cambridge, MA: Harvard University Press, 1999). See also Koen De Ceuster, "The World in a Book: Yu Kilchun's *Soyu kyonmun,*" in *Korea in the Middle: Korean Studies and Area Studies: Essays in Honour of Boudewijn Walraven,* ed. Remco E. Breuker (Leiden: CNWS Publications, 2008).

11. Michael E. Robinson, "Nationalism and the Korean Tradition, 1896–1920: Iconoclasm, Reform, and National Identity," *Korean Studies* 10, no. 1 (1986): 41.

12. Vipan Chandra, "Sentiment and Ideology in the Nationalism of the Independence Club (1896–1898)," *Korean Studies* 10 (1986): 23.

13. Chandra, 15.

14. Robinson, "Nationalism," 42.

15. Hillier to O'Conor, December 4, 1894. In Park Il-Keun, ed., *Anglo-American and Chinese Diplomatic Materials Relating to Korea, 1887–1897* (Seoul: Institute of Chinese Studies, Seoul National University, 1984), 484; here quoted from Kirk W. Larsen, "Competing Imperialisms in Korea," in *Routledge Handbook of Modern Korean History,* ed. Michael Seth (Abingdon, UK: Routledge, 2016), 34.

16. Yuanchong Wang, *Remaking the Chinese Empire: Manchu-Korean Relations, 1616–1911* (Ithaca, NY: Cornell University Press, 2018), 198.

17. Wang, *Remaking the Chinese Empire.*

18. Quan Hexiu, "The Chinese Press' Reporting and Commentary on Imperial Japan's Forced Annexation of the Taehan Empire," *International Journal of Korean History* 16, no. 2 (August 2011): 31–32.

19. Hexiu, 18–19.

20. Hexiu, 22.

21. Hexiu, 25.

22. For an overview, see Robinson, "Nationalism."

23. Han-Kyo Kim, "The Declaration of Independence, March 1, 1919: A New Translation," *Korean Studies* 13 (1989): 1–4.

24. Kim, "The Declaration of Independence."

25. President Wilson's Address to Congress, February 11, 1918, in *The Papers of Woodrow Wilson*, vol. 46: *January 16–March 12, 1918* (Princeton, NJ: Princeton University Press, 1984), 318.

26. See *Aleksandra Petrovna Kim-Stankevich: Ocherki, dokumenty i materialy* [Alexandra Petrovna Kim-Stankevich: Essays, documents and materials] (Moscow: Institut vostokovedeniia RAN, 2008). See also B. D Pak, *Borba Rossiiskikh Koreitsev Za Nezavisimost Korei, 1905–1919* [The struggle of Russian Koreans for the independence of Korea, 1905–1919], Rossiĭskie Koreĭtsy (Moscow: IV RAN, 2009).

27. On Chinese and Korean Communism in the early phase, see Hyun Ok Park, *Two Dreams in One Bed: Empire, Social Life, and the Origins of the North Korean Revolution in Manchuria* (Durham, NC: Duke University Press, 2005); and Zhihua Shen, "Sharing a Similar Fate: The Historical Process of the Korean Communists' Merger with the Chinese Communist Party (1919–1936)," *Journal of Modern Chinese History* 11, no. 1 (January 2017): 1–28.

28. On the Comintern and Korean Communism, see, in addition to Pak, *VKP(b), Komintern i Koreia, 1918–1941* [All-Union Communist Party (Bolsheviks), Comintern, and Korea, 1918–1941], ed. Wada Haruki and Kirill Shirinia (Moscow: ROSSPEN, 2007); and Vladimir Tikhonov, "'Korean Nationalism' Seen through the Comintern Prism, 1920s–30s," *Region: Regional Studies of Russia, Eastern Europe, and Central Asia* 6, no. 2 (2017): 201–224; and Vladimir Tikhonov and Kyounghwa Lim, "Communist Visions for Korea's Future: The 1920–30s," *Review of Korean Studies* 20, no. 1 (June 2017): 7–34. The classic account is Robert A. Scalapino and

Chong-Sik Lee, "The Origins of the Korean Communist Movement," pts. I and II, *Journal of Asian Studies* 20, no. 1 (1960): 9–31, and no. 2 (1961): 149–167.

29. "Da Yazhouzhuyi" [Great Asianism], in *Guofu quanji* [The complete works of the father of the nation] (Taipei: Jindai Zhongguo, 1989), 1:508–516; this translation based on https://en.wikisource.org/wiki/Sun_Yat-sen%27s _speech_on_Pan-Asianism. See also Craig A. Smith, "Chinese Asianism in the Early Republic: Guomindang Intellectuals and the Brief Internationalist Turn," *Modern Asian Studies* 53, no. 2 (March 2019): 582–605.

30. Thirty years later Chiang Kai-shek wrote an inscription praising the young man's action: "Yin Fengji zhi weiye yongchui buxiu: Jiang Jieshi xianshi bei gongkai" [Eternal glory to Yin Fengji's undertaking: Chiang Kai-shek's verse made public], *Zhongyang ribao*, December 19, 2013. Chiang wrote: "Know righteousness, know life and death."

31. See Bruce Cumings, *Korea's Place in the Sun: A Modern History* (New York: W. W. Norton, 2005), 174–184; Allyn Vannoy, "Korea under the Rising Sun," https://warfarehistorynetwork.com/daily/wwii/korea -under-the-rising-sun/.

32. Quoted from Howard W. French, *Everything under the Heavens: How the Past Helps Shape China's Push for Global Power* (Brunswick: Scribe, 2017), 72.

33. Quoted from Myongsob Kim and Seok Won Kim, "The Geopolitical Perceptions of Kim Ku and Syngman Rhee: Focusing on the Period of Japanese Occupation," *Korean Social Sciences Review* 1, no. 1 (2011): 124.

34. Kim and Kim, 133.

35. Xiaoyuan Liu, "Sino-American Diplomacy over Korea during World War II," *Journal of American–East Asian Relations* 1, no. 2 (1992): 240. See also Ku Daeyeol, "China's Policy toward Korea during World War II: Restoration of Power and the Korean Question," *Korea Journal* 43, no. 4 (2003): 215–239.

36. Liu, "Sino-American Diplomacy," 227.

37. Odd Arne Westad, *Cold War and Revolution: Soviet-American Rivalry and the Origins of the Chinese Civil War, 1944–1946* (New York: Columbia University Press, 1993).

38. "Record of a Meeting between T. V. Soong and Stalin," July 2, 1945, Cold War International History Program Digital Archive,

Woodrow Wilson Center (hereafter cited as CWIHP), http://digitalarchive
.wilsoncenter.org/document/122505.

39. Young Ick Lew, *The Making of the First Korean President: Syngman
Rhee's Quest for Independence, 1875–1948* (Honolulu: University of Hawai'i
Press, 2013), 275.

40. "Record of Conversation between Kim Gu and Liu Yuwan,"
July 11, 1948, CWIHP, http://digitalarchive.wilsoncenter.org/document
/119630.

41. Lew, *Making of the First Korean President*, 263.

42. South Korea also carried out land reform, but only later. There,
however, the peasants kept control of their land. See Inhan Kim, "Land
Reform in South Korea under the U.S. Military Occupation, 1945–1948,"
Journal of Cold War Studies 18, no. 2 (June 2016): 97–129.

43. On Chinese Communist assistance, see Donggil Kim, "Prelude
to War? The Repatriation of Koreans from the Chinese PLA, 1949–50,"
Cold War History 12, no. 2 (May 2012): 227–244.

44. Quoted in Donggil Kim, "New Insights into Mao's Initial Strategic Consideration towards the Korean War Intervention," *Cold War
History* 16, no. 3 (2016): 242–243.

45. Information from Yumi Moon, October 2019. Moon is preparing
an article on the subject.

46. For overviews of the Korean War from different perspectives,
see Bruce Cumings, *The Korean War: A History* (New York: Modern Library, 2011); Wada Haruki, *The Korean War: An International History*
(Lanham, MD: Rowman and Littlefield, 2014); William Stueck, *Rethinking the Korean War: A New Diplomatic and Strategic History* (Princeton,
NJ: Princeton University Press, 2004); and, for a broad perspective, Ha-
jimu Masuda, *Cold War Crucible: The Korean Conflict and the Postwar
World* (Cambridge, MA: Harvard University Press, 2015). For the origins
of the war on the Chinese side, see Chen Jian's classic *China's Road to the
Korean War: The Making of the Sino-American Confrontation* (New York:
Columbia University Press, 1994); and Niu Jun, "The Birth of the People's
Republic of China and the Road to the Korean War," in *The Cambridge
History of the Cold War*, ed. Melvyn P. Leffler and Odd Arne Westad
(Cambridge: Cambridge University Press, 2010), 1:221–243. Two China-
based scholars, Shen Zhihua and Kim Donggil, have helped transform

the study of the China's Korean war over the past years. For Shen, see *A Misunderstood Friendship: Mao Zedong, Kim Il-Sung, and Sino–North Korean Relations, 1949–1976* (New York: Columbia University Press, 2018); Shen, "China and the Dispatch of the Soviet Air Force: The Formation of the Chinese-Soviet-Korean Alliance in the Early Stage of the Korean War," *Journal of Strategic Studies* 33, no. 2 (2010): 211–230; Shen, *Mao Zedong, Sidalin yu Chaoxian zhanzheng* [Mao Zedong, Stalin, and the Korean War] (Guangzhou: Guangdong renmin, 2007). For Kim, see "China's Intervention in the Korean War Revisited," *Diplomatic History* 40, no. 5 (November 1, 2016): 1002–1026; and Kim, "New Insights."

47. Memorandum of Discussion at the 193d Meeting of the National Security Council, Tuesday, April 13, 1954, *Foreign Relations of the United States, 1952–1954,* Korea, vol. 15, pt. 2, 1787.

48. Xiaobing Li, *China's Battle for Korea: The 1951 Spring Offensive* (Bloomington: Indiana University Press, 2014), 54–55.

49. For an overview, see Balázs Szalontai, *Kim Il Sung in the Khrushchev Era: Soviet-DPRK Relations and the Roots of North Korean Despotism, 1953–1964* (Stanford, CA: Stanford University Press, 2005). See also Donggil Kim and Seong-hyon Lee, "Historical Perspective on China's 'Tipping Point' with North Korea," *Asian Perspective* 42, no. 1 (2018): 33–60; Andrei Lankov, "Kim Takes Control: The 'Great Purge' in North Korea, 1956–1960," *Korean Studies* 26, no. 1 (2002): 87–119; Andrei Lankov, *Crisis in North Korea: The Failure of Destalinization, 1956,* Hawai'i Studies on Korea (Honolulu: University of Hawai'i Press, 2004).

50. Telegram from the Department of State to the Embassy in Korea, Washington, April 23, 1960, *Foreign Relations of the United States, 1958–1960,* Japan, Korea, 18:637.

51. The word comes from a translation of the Marxist term "subject"—the one who acts within the objectively given range of possibilities.

52. Lyong Choi, "The Foreign Policy of Park Chunghee: 1968–1979" (PhD diss., London School of Economics and Political Science, 2012), 951.

53. Soviet embassy report, "The DPRK Attitude toward the So-Called 'Cultural Revolution' in China," March 7, 1967, CWIHP, https://digitalarchive.wilsoncenter.org/document/114570.

54. "Report, Embassy of Hungary in North Korea to the Hungarian Foreign Ministry," March 9, 1967, CWIHP, https://digitalarchive.wilson center.org/document/114578.

55. For an overview of economic development, see Young-Iob Chung, *South Korea in the Fast Lane: Economic Development and Capital Formation* (Oxford: Oxford University Press, 2007); Byung-Kook Kim and Ezra F. Vogel, eds., *The Park Chung Hee Era: The Transformation of South Korea* (Cambridge, MA: Harvard University Press, 2011); G. Brazinsky, *Nation Building in South Korea: Koreans, Americans, and the Making of a Democracy* (Chapel Hill, NC: University of North Carolina Press, 2007).

56. For Park's background, see Carter J. Eckert's superb biography, *Park Chung Hee and Modern Korea: The Roots of Militarism, 1866–1945* (Cambridge, MA: Harvard University Press, 2016).

57. For an overview, see Kim and Vogel, *Park Chung Hee Era*.

58. Choi, "Foreign Policy of Park Chunghee," 101.

59. Quoted in Yongho Kim, *North Korean Foreign Policy: Security Dilemma and Succession* (Lanham, MD: Lexington Books, 2010), 85.

60. Kim Il-sung, *With the Century* (Pyongyang: Foreign Languages Publishing House, 1998), 8:404.

3. China and Korea Today

1. Barbara Demick, *Nothing to Envy: Ordinary Lives in North Korea* (New York: Spiegel and Grau, 2010), 113.

2. The United States first stationed nuclear weapons in South Korea in 1958, and they were not withdrawn until 1991. South Korea sought to develop its own nuclear weapons program in the early 1970s, but it abandoned most of these efforts under US pressure when the ROK signed the Nonproliferation Treaty in 1975.

3. "Address before a Joint Session of the Congress on the State of the Union," February 4, 2002, https://www.govinfo.gov/app/details/WCPD -2002-02-04/WCPD-2002-02-04-Pg133-3.

4. Ji Hoon Park, Yong Suk Lee, and Hogeun Seo, "The Rise and Fall of Korean Drama Export to China: The History of State Regulation of Korean Dramas in China," *International Communication Gazette* 81, no. 2 (March 1, 2019): 139–157.

5. Evan Osnos, "Asia Rides Wave of Korean Pop Culture Invasion," *Chicago Tribune,* December 23, 2005.

6. For these figures, see Pew Research Center Global Trends, https://www.pewresearch.org/global/database/. In 2017 only 34 percent of South Koreans held a favorable view of China.

7. Quoted by *South China Morning Post,* September 4, 2017.

8. Quoted at Global Security, https://www.globalsecurity.org/wmd /library/news/dprk/2006/dprk-061004-kcna01.htm.

9. Information from interview with a former high-ranking Chinese official, Beijing.

10. The PRC-DPRK Mutual Aid and Cooperation Friendship Treaty, which is still in force, promises, "In the event of one of the Contracting Parties being subjected to the armed attack by any state or several states jointly and thus being involved in a state of war, the other Contracting Party shall immediately render military and other assistance by all means at its disposal." So, technically at least, China and North Korea are allies.

11. "Response to questions from Russia's ITAR-TASS news agency," October 13, 2011, http://naenara.com.kp/en/news/news_view.php?22+1477.

12. Kristin Huang, "How China Reacted to Previous North Korean Nuclear Tests," *South China Morning Post,* September 4, 2017.

13. This misapprehension is much helped by the fact that the two countries have distinct names in Chinese: Chaoxian (Chosŏn) for North Korea, and Hanguo for the South.

14. *Washington Post,* February 23, 2017.

15. Associated Press report, April 27, 2017.

16. Quoted in Katsuji Nakazawa, "Mao Zedong and the Roots of the North Korea Nuclear Crisis," *Nikkei Asian Review,* January 1, 2018.

17. *New York Times,* April 18, 2017.

18. For Trump's statement, see https://abcnews.go.com/Politics/trump -north-korea-met-fire-fury-threats-continue/story?id=49097627. The North Korean statement had said, "The U.S. is feeling uneasy . . . because its hostile policy will end in [futility] when the DPRK conducts the test-fire of ICBM capable of precisely striking any place on the U.S. mainland" (https:// abcnews.go.com/International/fire-fury-rocket-man-barbs-traded-trump -kim/story?id=53634996).

19. Uri Friedman, "North Korea Says It Has 'Completed' Its Nuclear Program," *The Atlantic*, November 29, 2017, https://www.theatlantic.com /international/archive/2017/11/north-korea-nuclear/547019/.

Conclusion

1. Or, as Brook, Walt van Praag, and Boltjes put it, "'Sovereignty,' when the term is applied in Asian history, was mostly divisible, layered, and relative, as were allegiance, loyalty, and subjection" (Timothy Brook, M. C. van Walt van Praag, and Miek Boltjes, *Sacred Mandates: Asian International Relations since Chinggis Khan* (Chicago: University of Chicago Press, 2018), 15.

2. Of course, even in Europe the Westphalian system was often more theory than practice.

3. For more on this for the early twentieth century, see André Schmid, "Decentering the 'Middle Kingdom': The Problem of China in Korean Nationalist Thought, 1895–1910," in *Nation Work: Asian Elites and National Identities*, ed. Timothy Brook and André Schmid (Ann Arbor: University of Michigan Press, 2000), 83–107.

4. Most recently brought to fame by Xi Jinping's statement that "shixian zhonghua minzu weida fuxing shi zhonghua minzu jindai yilai zui weida de mengxiang"[the great rejuvenation of the Chinese nation is the greatest dream of the Chinese nation in modern times]. See Xi's speech on November 29, 2012, at http://cpc.people.com.cn/xuexi/n/2015 /0717/c397563-27322292.html.

5. Choe Sang-Hun, "North Korea Urgently Needs Food Aid after Worst Harvest in Decade, U.N. Says," *New York Times*, May 4, 2019.

ACKNOWLEDGMENTS

I am very grateful to those who helped out with this project and with its transformation into a book. Michael Szonyi first invited me to give the Edwin O. Reischauer Lectures for 2017, and the staff at Harvard's Fairbank Center for Chinese Study helped organize them. Ezra F. Vogel, Kirk W. Larsen, and Sung-yoon Lee, respectively, commented on each of the lectures; Gregg Brazinsky, Carter Eckert, and Yumi Moon read the whole manuscript and provided extremely helpful advice. Kim Donggil, Niu Jun, Chen Jian, Niu Ke, Niu Dayong, Shen Zhihua, Li Danhui, Wang Dong, Li Chen, as well as my students Hahn Kwan Woo and Dong-Hyeon Kim, helped with parts of the text, and the History Department at Peking University, the Korea Foundation for Advanced Studies in Seoul, and the Sigur Center for Asian Studies at George Washington University invited me to present early drafts of the manuscript. As always, I am grateful to my literary agent Sarah Chalfant at the Wylie Agency, and it has been a pleasure to work with Kathleen McDermott and the staff at Harvard University Press throughout this project. Sarah Masotta did much to help out at Yale's Jackson Institute for Global Affairs, and Kelly Sandefer and Beehive Mapping produced excellent maps. My former student Choi Lyong, now a professor at the Korea Military Academy, has taught me a lot about his country. One of the most helpful discussions of the project took place in the Korean Students' Association of Peking University during my 2019 tenure as Boeing Company Chair in International Relations at Schwarzman College, across the street at Tsinghua University. The book is dedicated to the united, peaceful Korea of the future that Korean students in Beijing and elsewhere so fervently wish for.

INDEX

Akkadian empire, 9

Boltjes, Miek, 193n1
Britain, 16, 20, 67–69, 71
Brook, Timothy, 15, 193n1
Buddhism, 6
Burbank, Jane, 176n6
Bush, George W., 139–140, 144, 147

Ch'eng, Chung-ying, 25
Chiang Kai-shek, 98–99, 102, 103–104, 108, 119, 188n30
China, 5–6; cultural overlap with Korea, 6–7; as culture, 175n1; as empire, 10–14; Korea relations, overview, 14, 161–166; nationalism in, 89, 163–164. *See also* Guomindang; Ming empire; People's Republic of China; Qing empire
Chinese Communist Party (CCP): establishment of PRC, 109;

Guomindang and, 97, 98, 103–104, 105–106; hold on power, 134; Korean Communists and, 95–96, 104–105, 106–107. *See also* Mao Zedong; People's Republic of China
Cho Pong-am, 123
Ch'oe Che-u, 73
Chŏng To-jŏn, 32
Chongzhen (Ming emperor), 62
Chosŏn state: administrative organization, 32, 34; Christianity and, 67, 69, 72–73, 185n86; complex sovereignty of, 162; cultural conservatism and self-containment, 63–64, 72, 184n80, 184n82; establishment, 8–9, 31; First Sino-Japanese War and, 81–82; intellectual exchange with China, 45–46, 65; Japan, annexation by, 87–89; Japan, Imjin War with, 49–56; Japan relations and pressure, 38,

197

Republic of Korea (ROK).
See South Korea
reunification, Korean, 2–3, 127,
129–130, 131–132, 141, 160, 167, 171
Rhee, Syngman (Yi Sŭng-man):
on Communism in South
Korea, 109; in exile and provisional government, 90, 96–97,
102, 106; leadership by, 107–108,
118–119, 123; reunification and,
112; US and, 106, 118–119, 121, 123
righteous armies (*ŭibyŏng*), 23,
52–53, 91, 179n35
righteousness: definition, 22; Korea
and, 22–23, 26, 59–60, 83–84;
neo-Confucianism and, 23–26
Robinson, Ronald, 16
Roh Tae-woo, 131, 132
Roman empire, 10
Roosevelt, Franklin, 103
Russia, 85. *See also* Soviet Union
Russo-Japanese War, 86–87

sadae (serving the great), 35–36,
38, 83
Seoul, 34, 50, 118, 150, 173
Shen Zhihua, 189n46
Shenbao (newspaper), 89
Shibao (newspaper), 89
singularity, compound, 163
Sino-Japanese War, First, 81–82
Sino-Korean Mutual Assistance
Association, 96
Sino-Korean relations, approach
to, 3–4. *See also* China; Korea
sirhak (practical learning), 65, 69

Six-Party Talks, 143, 144, 147, 149,
168
Song empire, 8, 14–15, 23
Song Ziwen, 105
Sŏnjo (Chosŏn king), 49, 52, 55–56
South Korea (ROK): challenges
facing, 169; China relations, 130,
132, 140–141, 143–144, 151–152,
155–156, 165, 166–167; Communist uprisings, 109; democratic
governments, 131, 140; economic
advances, 2, 127–128, 134, 140;
establishment, 108–109; land
reforms, 122, 189n42; name, 121,
176n7; North Korea relations,
136–137, 144, 149–150; nuclear
program, 191n2; Park's leadership, 128–129; rebuilding after
Korean War, 121–122; reunification and, 112, 129–130, 131–132,
160, 167; Rhee's leadership,
107–108, 118–119, 123; Soviet relations, 132; Sunshine Policy, 144;
Terminal High Altitude Area
Defense (THAAD) and, 155–156
sovereignty, complex, 162, 193n1
Soviet Union (USSR): Bolshevik
Revolution's impact on Korea,
94–95; China relations, 120,
124–125; Korean War and,
112–113; liberation of Korea and,
104–106; North Korea relations,
110, 118, 121–122, 129; nuclear
program in North Korea and,
138; South Korea relations, 132.
See also Russia